W. E. B.
DU BOIS

W. E. B. DU BOIS

Mark Stafford

Senior Consulting Editor
Nathan Irvin Huggins
Director
*W.E.B. Du Bois Institute for Afro-American Research
Harvard University*

CHELSEA HOUSE PUBLISHERS
New York   Philadelphia

CHELSEA HOUSE PUBLISHERS
Editor-in-Chief Nancy Toff
Executive Editor Remmel T. Nunn
Managing Editor Karyn Gullen Browne
Copy Chief Juliann Barbato
Picture Editor Adrian G. Allen
Art Director Maria Epes
Manufacturing Manager Gerald Levine

Black Americans of Achievement
Senior Editor Richard Rennert

Staff for W. E. B. DU BOIS
Copy Editor Brian Sookram
Deputy Copy Chief Nicole Bowen
Editorial Assistant Navorn Johnson
Picture Researcher Amla Sanghvi
Assistant Art Director Loraine Machlin
Designer Ghila Krajzman
Production Coordinator Joseph Romano
Cover Illustration Daniel Mark Duffy

First Printing

1 3 5 7 9 8 6 4 2

Library of Congress Cataloging-in-Publication Data
Stafford, Mark.
W. E. B. DuBois.
(Black Americans of achievement)
Bibliography: p.
Includes index.
Summary: Examines the life of the black scholar and leader who
devoted himself to gaining equality for his people.
1. Du Bois, W. E. B. (William Edward Burghardt), 1868–
1963—Juvenile literature.   2. Afro-Americans—Biography—
Juvenile literature.   [1. Du Bois, W. E. B. (William Edward
Burghardt), 1868–1963.   2. Civil rights workers. 3. Afro-
Americans—Biography]   I. Title.
II. Series.
E185.97.D73S68   1989   303.48'4'092   [B] [92]   89-9705

ISBN 1-55546-582-X.
   0-7910-0238-1 (pbk.)

CONTENTS

———— ❦ ————

BLACK
AMERICANS
OF
ACHIEVEMENT

Muhammad Ali
heavyweight champion

Richard Allen
*founder of the
African Methodist
Episcopal church*

Louis Armstrong
musician

James Baldwin
author

Benjamin Banneker
*scientist and
mathematician*

Mary McLeod Bethune
educator

Blanche K. Bruce
politician

Ralph Bunche
diplomat

George Washington Carver
botanist

Charles Waddell Chestnutt
author

Paul Cuffe
merchant and abolitionist

Frederick Douglass
abolitionist editor

Charles R. Drew
physician

W.E.B. Du Bois
scholar and activist

Paul Laurence Dunbar
poet

Duke Ellington
bandleader and composer

Ralph Ellison
author

Ella Fitzgerald
singer

Marcus Garvey
black-nationalist leader

Prince Hall
social reformer

William H. Hastie
educator and politician

Matthew A. Henson
explorer

Chester Himes
author

Billie Holiday
singer

John Hope
educator

Lena Horne
entertainer

Langston Hughes
poet

James Weldon Johnson
author

Scott Joplin
composer

Martin Luther King, Jr.
civil rights leader

Joe Louis
heavyweight champion

Malcolm X
militant black leader

Thurgood Marshall
Supreme Court justice

Elijah Muhammad
religious leader

Jesse Owens
champion athlete

Gordon Parks
photographer

Sidney Poitier
actor

Adam Clayton Powell, Jr.
political leader

A. Philip Randolph
labor leader

Paul Robeson
singer and actor

Jackie Robinson
baseball great

John Russwurm
publisher

Sojourner Truth
antislavery activist

Harriet Tubman
antislavery activist

Nat Turner
slave revolt leader

Denmark Vesey
slave revolt leader

Madame C. J. Walker
entrepreneur

Booker T. Washington
educator

Walter White
political activist

Richard Wright
author

ON
ACHIEVEMENT

Coretta Scott King

BEFORE YOU BEGIN this book, I hope you will ask yourself what the word excellence means to you. I think that it's a question we should all ask, and keep asking as we grow older and change. Because the truest answer to it should never change. When you think of excellence, perhaps you think of success at work; or of becoming wealthy; or meeting the right person, getting married, and having a good family life.

Those important goals are worth striving for, but there is a better way to look at excellence. As Martin Luther King, Jr., said in one of his last sermons, "I want you to be first in love. I want you to be first in moral excellence. I want you to be first in generosity. If you want to be important, wonderful. If you want to be great, wonderful. But recognize that he who is greatest among you shall be your servant."

My husband, Martin Luther King, Jr., knew that the true meaning of achievement is service. When I met him, in 1952, he was already ordained as a Baptist preacher and was working towards a doctoral degree at Boston University. I was studying at the New England Conservatory and dreamed of accomplishments in music. We married a year later, and after I graduated the following year we moved to Montgomery, Alabama. We didn't know it then, but our notions of achievement were about to undergo a dramatic change.

You may have read or heard about what happened next. What began with the boycott of a local bus line grew into a national movement, and by the time he was assassinated in 1968 my husband had fashioned a black movement powerful enough to shatter forever the practice of racial segregation. What you may not have read about is where he got his method for resisting injustice without compromising his religious beliefs.

He adopted the strategy of nonviolence from a man of a different race, who lived in a distant country, and even practiced a different religion. The man was Mahatma Gandhi, the great leader of India, who devoted his life to serving humanity in the spirit of love and nonviolence. It was in these principles that Martin discovered his method for social reform. More than anything else, those two principles were the key to his achievements.

This book is about black Americans who served society through the excellence of their achievements. It forms a part of the rich history of black men and women in America—a history of stunning accomplishments in every field of human endeavor, from literature and art to science, industry, education, diplomacy, athletics, jurisprudence, even polar exploration.

Not all of the people in this history had the same ideals, but I think you will find something that all of them have in common. Like Martin Luther King, Jr., they all decided to become "drum majors" and serve humanity. In that principle—whether it was expressed in books, inventions, or song—they found something outside themselves to use as a goal and a guide. Something that showed them a way to serve others, instead of living only for themselves.

Reading the stories of these courageous men and women not only helps us discover the principles that we will use to guide our own lives but also teaches us about our black heritage and about America itself. It is crucial for us to know the heroes and heroines of our history and to realize that the price we paid in our struggle for equality in America was dear. But we must also understand that we have gotten as far as we have partly because America's democratic system and ideals made it possible.

We are still struggling with racism and prejudice. But the great men and women in this series are a tribute to the spirit of our democratic ideals and the system in which they have flourished. And that makes their stories special and worth knowing. ◆

W. E. B.
DU BOIS

1

"TO BE
A LEADER
OF MY PEOPLE"

W. E. B. DU BOIS was eager to return home. After spending the last two years overseas, studying on a fellowship at Friedrich Wilhelm University in Berlin, Germany, he was ready to go back to the United States and put his education to work. In Berlin, where he had mixed freely with whites and had been treated as their equal, the black scholar had written in his diary that his chief aim was "to make a name for myself in science and literature and to be a leader of my people." Now, at the age of 26, the time to realize his goals had arrived.

Du Bois stepped onto the main deck of the SS *Chester* just as it began to veer into New York harbor. He was fairly bored after nine monotonous days at sea and decided to study the passengers who shared his steerage accommodations. Russians, Greeks, Austrians, Germans, Poles—they were an impressive sight.

It was the spring of 1894, and America had recently opened its doors to great waves of emigrants from eastern and southern Europe. Of the 800 passengers on the *Chester*, 350 were men, women, and children from the lower classes—farmers whose faces were bronzed and wrinkled from long days spent under the Mediterranean sun, pale workers who had sweated long hours in dim factories to pay their pas-

Du Bois at the Paris Exposition, a world's fair held in 1900, shortly after he became professor of history and economics at Atlanta University and began publishing a series of sociological studies of black life. He went on to become America's premier human rights leader for the first half of the century.

11

sage to the United States. All strained for glimpses of their new homeland.

Du Bois felt drawn to the "picturesque and laughable crowd . . . this great stream of hopes and longing," as he later described his fellow passengers in *The Autobiography of W. E. B. Du Bois*. In only one other place had he seen faces so deeply grooved with poverty and struggle: in the American South. There, as a college student at Fisk University in Nashville, Tennessee, he had observed the daily struggle of black sharecroppers.

To the immigrants on board the *Chester*, the black passenger clad in a smart European suit seemed poised to resume a prosperous life of which they could only dream. Yet Du Bois faced an uncertain future. He had only two dollars in the pockets of his neatly pressed trousers, and despite being brilliantly educated and a scholar of unusual promise, he had no immediate job prospects. Indeed, he rather envied the motley throng of newcomers. They envisioned a shining future in America. He, however, was returning to a land that offered little to himself or any other black.

"We wanted Life to end and begin," Du Bois later said of the passengers aboard the ship. In that respect, he felt a sense of kinship with the immigrants. Like them, he had resolved to wrest something from America. And like them, he threw himself into his mission with unflagging energy.

Upon arriving in New York City, Du Bois fired off letters to nearly every black university in the country. He found a job later that summer at Wilberforce University in Ohio, where he taught Latin and Greek to black students. From there he moved on to the University of Pennsylvania, where he joined the sociology faculty. One year later, he landed a long-term post at Atlanta University, whose president encouraged him to carry out a wide-ranging social study.

Booker T. Washington, the nation's leading black spokesman at the turn of the century, called on blacks to delay their campaign for political, social, and intellectual equality and concentrate chiefly on making economic gains. His accommodationist policies deeply upset Du Bois, who wrote in "Of Mr. Booker T. Washington and Others," an essay published in 1903, "We have no right to sit silently by while the inevitable seeds are sown for a harvest of disaster to our children, black or white."

Du Bois's main project at Atlanta University was a thorough examination of the problems faced by black Americans. His findings, which were issued annually beginning in 1898 as the *Atlanta University Publications on the Study of Negro Problems*, earned him a reputation as one of the leading black scholars in the United States. His renown was buttressed by other writings, including *The Philadelphia Negro*, an exhaustive study of a black community that was released in 1899, and *The Souls of Black Folk*, a series of incisive essays written with tremendous literary flair and published to critical acclaim in 1903.

But these triumphs did not give Du Bois what he coveted most: a position of great influence in the black community. He longed to attain this status not only because of the prestige it would confer on him but also because he was deeply troubled by the direction black leadership had taken around the turn of the century. His displeasure focused on the most celebrated black figure of the time, Booker T. Washington, a man who differed from Du Bois in practically every imaginable way.

Whereas Du Bois had grown up in a quiet Massachussetts town with few blacks and very few overt signs of racism, Washington had been reared in Virginia just after the Civil War—a time when southern blacks suffered miserably at the hands of their white neighbors. This essential difference between the two men led to many others. Du Bois's intellectual ambitions had been fed by local white leaders, and he enrolled in Fisk University on the strength of a scholarship. Washington entered college with a mop and pail; only by working as a janitor could he afford to squeeze in a few courses.

A gifted intellectual, Du Bois mastered the classic works of Western literature and history, first at Fisk, then as both an undergraduate and graduate student at Harvard University (where he was heaped with honors), and finally as a postgraduate scholar in Germany. Washington, for his part, applied himself to earthier issues, especially the difficulties that southern black sharecroppers faced in farming their meager plots of land. This matter, which held the key to black progress in the South, contributed greatly to Washington's rise as the nation's leading black spokesman.

After becoming the principal of Tuskegee Institute in Alabama, Washington argued that black sharecroppers could never escape from debt because the land they tilled and the farming methods they practiced were equally poor. Victims of poverty, they had no choice but to look to white landowners and lawmakers for help. Southern whites thus gained the authority to deal with blacks as they saw fit, and in many cases they treated blacks brutally.

Washington held that there was only one way for black Americans to escape from this cruel cycle: They had to eliminate their dependence on whites. And they could manage that only after they acquired industrial skills. This strategy became the cornerstone of Washington's program for racial progress for blacks.

Du Bois did not quarrel with Washington's contention that blacks needed to improve their labor skills to become a more integral part of the nation's economy. But he did diverge from Washington on another issue. As modest as the Tuskegee principal's aims were, they kindled the wrath of many southerners, especially poor white farmers who feared blacks would put them out of business. Washington, wary of these opponents, tried to placate white America by urging blacks not to agitate for equal rights. That would come in time, he said, after blacks became an indispensable part of the nation's economy. In the meantime, blacks should adopt the passive, humble stereotype that whites found nonthreatening.

This last tactic troubled Du Bois. He admired Washington and agreed with his emphasis on economic growth, but he felt that by cautioning blacks to assuage whites, Washington perpetuated the view that blacks were an inferior people. This notion galled Du Bois, who belonged to an elite group of blacks that had begun to make inroads into American society precisely because they defied the comfortable stereotypes cherished by white bigots. Du Bois believed that the black elite—members of the black middle class—should enlist their influence, wealth, and knowledge to improve the lot of other blacks.

Du Bois had a powerful argument, but he failed to secure much support for it—a fact that frustrated him to no end. No matter how many eloquent books he published and how much critics praised them, his influence did not radiate beyond the confines of America's small community of liberal thinkers and writers. To many blacks, Washington seemed rooted in the soil of hardship, whereas Du Bois was isolated in the ivory tower of his own intellect. As aloof as he was gifted, Du Bois was not a dynamic political leader. His ideas commanded attention, but most blacks tended not to follow his advice on racial matters.

One issue that troubled all black Americans was lynching, a horrific crime that violated every notion of law and justice. In turn-of-the-century America,

"Be the truth what it may," Du Bois wrote in his diary when he was 25, "I shall seek it on the pure assumption that it is worth seeking—and Heaven nor Hell, God nor Devil shall turn me from my purpose till I die." Shortly after he embarked on a career as a social scientist, however, he discovered that "there cut across this plan of science a red ray of emotion which could not be ignored."

Du Bois in his Atlanta University office in 1909, around the time when he was preparing to leave the school and play a more visible role in black affairs. He later said, "I faced situations which called—shrieked for action, even before any detailed, scientific study could possibly be prepared. I saw before me a problem that could not await the last word of science, but demanded immediate action to prevent social death."

a week did not pass without a black man being murdered by a mob of whites quick to take the law into their own bloodthirsty hands and act against alleged felons. Like all blacks, Washington was deeply troubled by these attacks and tried to develop ways of fighting them. Yet he had assured whites that the "negro was . . . peace loving" and would refrain from staging any public protests. In fact, Washington had made a commitment to that effect.

To Du Bois, such passivity was intolerable in the face of such evil. But he did not have an immediate answer to the lynching problem, either. Since his university days, he had believed that the scientific study of the black community would lead to understanding and social improvements. Such study had led to his path-breaking books. But what good had they done? Blacks were still dying, and no hope glimmered.

Du Bois saw only one solution. Blacks, as a group, must demand their right to fair treatment before the law. Accordingly, they must lobby for full recognition as American citizens.

One day in 1903, Du Bois decided to put his plan into action. A black man named Sam Hose had been

arrested in central Georgia for murdering his landlord
and raping the man's wife. The possibility that a black
man had harmed a white woman was what usually lit
the fuse of lynch mobs, and Hose was an obvious
candidate for their hangman's noose.

Du Bois, determined that Hose should receive a
fair trial, banked on his own renown in calling attention to the case and stopping the mob. He sum-
moned his powers of intellect and, as he later stated
in his autobiography, "wrote a careful and reasoned
statement concerning the evident facts and started
down to the *Atlanta Constitution* office." The newspaper, he was sure, would present the facts of the
case to members of the local white community and
calm their anger.

Normally, DuBois disliked setting foot outside the
Atlanta University campus. This aversion was a form
of protest: He tried to avoid any place where racial
segregation was practiced. On this occasion, however, he violated his own policy and set off for the
newspaper office.

But before Du Bois reached his destination, "news
met me," he later wrote. "Sam Hose had been
lynched, and they said his knuckles were on exhi-
bition at a grocery store farther down on Mitchell
Street, along which I was walking. I turned back to
the university." Busy penning his statement to the
press, he had arrived too late for it to do any good.

The image of the lynch mob etched in Du Bois's
mind all that was wrong with the plight of black
Americans and colored it with a grim hue. No longer
would scholarship suffice as his principal means of
inspiring others. If he meant to better the condition
of blacks, he had to guide them along the path of
action. And to do that, he had to become a much
more vocal leader. ◆

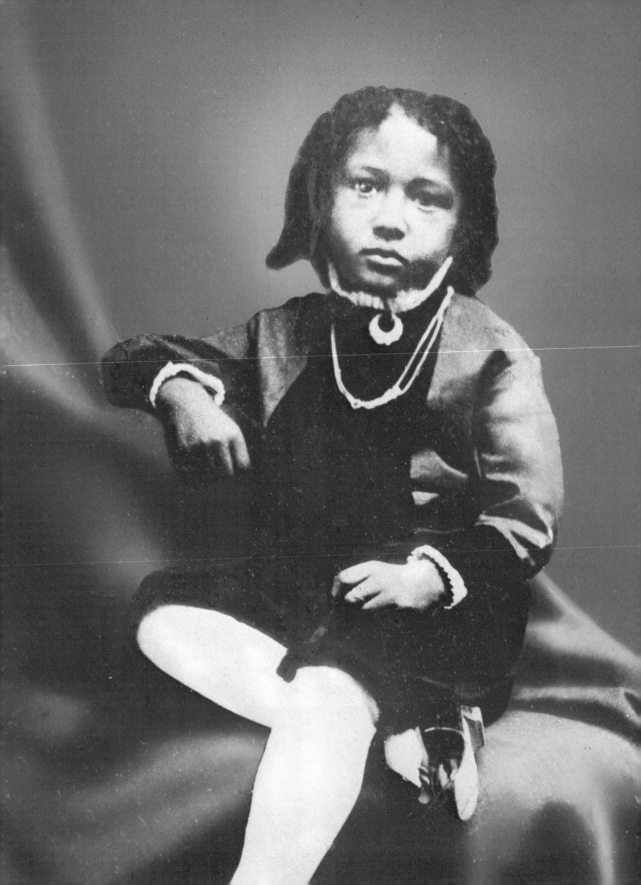

2

"A BOY'S PARADISE"

WILLIAM EDWARD BURGHARDT Du Bois was born on February 23, 1868, in a small clapboard house on Church Street in Great Barrington, Massachusetts. Surrounded by the Berkshire hills, Great Barrington was an idyllic middle-class community boasting tree-lined streets with white picket fences. The town experienced so little crime that it needed just one policeman.

Of the rural community's 5,000 inhabitants, only about 50 were black. The rest of the population was composed of Irish and Dutch immigrants and the descendants of New England Puritans. "Standing did not depend on what the ancestor did, or who he was, but rather that he existed, lived decently and thus linked the individual to the community," Du Bois wrote of his birthplace in his autobiography.

His mother's family, the Burghardts, was one of the oldest clans in Great Barrington, black or white. William's great-great-grandfather Tom was born in West Africa about 1730 and seized as a child by a Dutch slave trader, Conraet Burghardt, who brought the boy to Berkshire County. By the time Tom died 50 years later, Massachusetts had adopted a Bill of Rights, which stated that all people in the commonwealth were free.

A prosperous farming family, Tom's descendants found themselves in an unusual position when com-

Du Bois at the age of four. "I had a pleasant childhood," he later said. "I can remember no poverty although my family was certainly poor."

pared with most blacks in America, who were poor and enslaved. Yet the black Burghardts were not completely integrated into white society. "The color line," Du Bois wrote in his autobiography, "was manifest and yet not absolutely drawn." Consequently, his ancestors developed a strong sense of racial pride and independence.

In 1831, one of Tom's grandsons, Othello, and his wife, Sarah, had the last of their dozen or so children, Mary Salvina Burghardt. Sheltered by her overly protective family, she led a quiet life and became a housemaid. Then, in 1867, a handsome, light-skinned man known as Alfred Du Bois arrived in Great Barrington.

Alfred was partly of French ancestry. His grandfather, Dr. James Du Bois, was a white plantation owner in the Bahamas who had sired two sons with one of his slaves. Both boys were pale skinned, and their father decided to treat them as his own and gave them a proper education. Alexander, the eldest, was sent to a private school in Connecticut, where he was treated as though he were white. But when his father died, he became the responsibility of an indifferent cousin who decided that Alexander should be regarded as black. The youth was promptly removed from school and apprenticed to a shoemaker.

Alexander rebelled against this change in fortune and spent the balance of his life seeking to recover his former status as a white gentleman. A restless wanderer, he went from Connecticut to the black republic of Haiti and then back to Connecticut before settling in southwestern Massachusetts. During his many travels, he married three times and had four children. One of them, born in 1825, was a son named Alfred.

Alfred—small and handsome, with wavy hair—was cut from the same cloth as his father. Something of a vagabond poet, he loved literature deeply and

Du Bois's paternal grandfather, Alexander, was a mulatto (he was born in the Bahamas to a black mother and white father) burdened by his mixed racial heritage; he regarded himself as neither black nor white and spent most of his life attempting to find his place in the world. In contrast, the other side of Du Bois's family, the Burghardts, was one of the oldest clans in Great Barrington, Massachusetts.

possessed a desire to travel. In 1867, he arrived in Great Barrington with few prospects. Yet he quickly won Mary Burghardt's heart, despite her family's protests to her that he was not respectable.

As it turned out, the protests were well founded. Shortly after William was born in 1868, Alfred left for New Milford, Connecticut, a town 40 miles south of Great Barrington. There, in a place far removed from Mary's domineering family, he was supposed to establish a home for his wife and only son. He had promised to write for them once he was settled, but his letter failed to arrive, and Mary and William never saw or heard from him again.

Apart from this separation, William's early childhood was surprisingly free of strife. "The little family of my mother and myself must often have been near the edge of poverty," he wrote in his autobiography. "Yet I was not hungry or in lack of suitable clothing

Du Bois's parents were a pair of opposites whose marriage did not last for long. His mother, Mary (right), came from an earnest and hardworking New England family—"she was rather silent, but very determined and very patient," Du Bois said—whereas his father, Alfred (opposite), "had in him the making of a poet, an adventurer, or a Beloved Vagabond." About a year after Du Bois was born, Alfred left his wife and child for good.

and shoes, or made to feel unfortunate." Growing up in what he called "a boy's paradise," he often played in the woods and caves of the Berkshire hills and along the banks of the "golden" Housatonic River, whose gorgeous color, he eventually discovered, was the result of pollution from the mills that it powered.

Mary and William lived with Grandfather Burghardt on the outskirts of Great Barrington for almost five years, until Othello died in 1873. Then mother and son moved to the center of town, where Mary once again took up work as a domestic. William enrolled in public school the following year.

Academic work clearly agreed with him. The work ethic that the Burghardts had passed on to Wil-

liam helped him become an excellent student. In the crowded wooden schoolhouse, he was promoted ahead of the other children his age.

The fact that William was black and virtually all of his classmates were white made little difference to his educators, who often embraced him as the "teacher's pet." The brown color of his skin also made little difference to William, at least for a while. "I was as a boy long unconscious of color discrimination in any obvious and specific way," he wrote in his autobiography. Yet the realities of racial prejudice slowly began to enter his life.

One day, William and some of his white friends were playing a game in which they exchanged calling cards, which was something their parents did when they made social calls. William offered his card to a white girl who had recently moved to town, but she refused to accept it. Shaken from his insulated world, he was aware from then on that his skin color marked him as an outcast. "I found it difficult and even unnecessary to approach other people," he said, "and by that same token my own inner life perhaps grew the richer."

The resultant sense of rejection also increased William's desire to succeed, and he proceeded to study harder than ever before. His mother, who had not received any formal schooling, wanted him to accomplish much more than she had and kept on reminding him, he said, that "there was no real discrimination on account of color—it was all a matter of ability and hard work." It was a philosophy with which William could find little fault. "I found it easy to excel most of my classmates in studies," he said. "The secret of life and loosing the color bar, then, lay in excellence, in accomplishment."

Yet there was an occasional setback. While William was growing up, his mother suffered a paralytic stroke that left her lame in one leg and with a crippled left hand. She was not able to work as often after the onset of the illness. Accordingly, the Burghardts and their neighbors attempted to help out Mary and her son whenever they could. Aunts and uncles joined forces with local white families to provide William and his mother with money to buy shoes and books.

William pitched in as well, delivering groceries, shoveling coal, chopping wood, mowing lawns, hawking newspapers. He was as deeply attached to his mother as she was to him, and he took great pride in trying to make her life as comfortable as possible. On those occasions when she was able to work, he met her at the end of the day and walked her home, arm in arm.

Mary Burghardt Du Bois holds her newborn son, William, in 1868. "The year of my birth," he later noted, "was the year that the freedmen of the South were enfranchised, and for the first time as a mass took part in government."

By the time William entered Great Barrington High School in 1881, he had become, as he later put it, "thrown in upon myself." A dutiful churchgoer, he had managed to adopt the reserved Calvinist air that was characteristic of many New Englanders and had learned to avoid any situation where there was even the slightest hint of racial discrimination. Moreover, his school offered few opportunities for social activity. This was partly because his high school had an enrollment of just 25 students. Most of the rural community's teenagers had to discontinue their formal education at an early age so they could help out on the family farm.

One of William's favorite ways of spending his free time was browsing at a local bookstore owned by Johnny Morgan. The bookseller took an interest in the promising young student, and when William was in his second year of high school, Morgan allowed the 14 year old to buy a set of history books on credit. These volumes proved to be so valuable to William that he kept them for the rest of his life.

Morgan also helped William land a part-time job selling subscriptions for a black newspaper, the *New York Globe*. Shortly thereafter, William, who coedited his school newspaper, the *Howler*, also became, at age 15, the *Globe*'s Great Barrington correspondent and a reporter for the *Springfield Republican*. He suggested in his articles that the public contact him to find out what were the best books to read. He also urged the local black community to attend town meetings and take an active part in local politics. William had begun to go to these meetings, which were characterized by lengthy orations and debates, when he was around 13 years old.

A trip in 1883 to Rocky Point, Rhode Island, for an annual picnic attended by thousands of black families from New York, Connecticut, and Massachusetts piqued William's interest in black affairs. There he observed "Negroes of every hue and bearing, saw in opened-mouth astonishment the whole gorgeous gamut of the American Negro; the swaggering men, the beautiful girls, the laughter and gaiety, the unhampered self-expression. I was astonished and inspired." It was a striking introduction to a world beyond his own, a world to which he belonged more firmly than to the community of Great Barrington—the world of color.

Before long, William formed the Sons of Freedom, a small club dedicated to the "advancement of the colored race" in Great Barrington. Members of the club were expected to attend lectures, study

American history, and take part in debates. Like his news articles, the activities of the Sons of Freedom affirmed his growing belief that blacks needed to organize if they wanted to win their civil rights.

William and a dozen other students graduated from Great Barrington High School in 1884. The lone black in his class—and the first black ever to graduate from the school—he gave a commencement address on the abolitionist Wendell Phillips, who had died earlier in the year. The rousing applause that William's speech received went a long way in encouraging him to speak out on injustice and ignorance in the coming years.

William's immediate goal, though, was to go to college—a substantial ambition for any poor youth in late-19th-century America, black or white. Moreover, he wanted to attend Harvard College, which was located directly across the state in Cambridge, Massachusetts, and was widely regarded as one of the best schools in the country. As one of the few students in his graduating class who planned to continue his formal education, William became something of a prize pupil to all of Great Barrington.

As a result, four townspeople—Frank Hosmer, the high school principal; Edward Van Lennep, prin-

Du Bois spent his early years in this house in Great Barrington, Massachusetts. "The town," he observed, "was shut in by its mountains and provincialism."

Du Bois (far left) with the Great Barrington High School graduating class of 1884. Frank Hosmer (front row, center), the school principal, played a major role in raising money for Du Bois to attend college.

cipal of the local private school; and the Reverends C. C. Painter and Evarts Scudder—labored to set up a scholarship for Du Bois. They urged him to spend a year working and brushing up on his studies while they raised the money for his college tuition, and William agreed. He spent the year after high school as a timekeeper on a construction project, where he learned a bit about workers' rights.

In the summer of 1885, Du Bois was told that enough money had been raised for him to attend Fisk University in Nashville, Tennessee. Established in 1866 as a school for blacks, it aimed at becoming one of the best educational institutions in the South. But Fisk was not Harvard. William's mother and his relatives, who were all extremely proud of his academic accomplishments, grew angry that he was not remaining in the North and was being sent to a part of the country where slavery had been a way of life.

Du Bois, too, was disappointed that he was not going to Harvard. Yet the South held a special appeal for him. "I was going to meet colored people of my own age and education, of my own ambitions," he said. Blacks in the South lived in a segregated society. They were denied the right to vote, were prevented from holding public office, and found it difficult to escape from dire poverty. But if he wanted to be a leader of his people, the South, he knew, was the place to begin. "Black folk," he said, "were bound in time to play a large role in the South."

Half a year before the 17-year-old Du Bois set out for Fisk, his mother died. Her love and encouragement had nourished his ambition and early success, and she had relied on him a great deal. Her death, as great a blow as it was to William, made the thought of leaving Great Barrington easier for him to bear.

In September 1885, Du Bois embarked on the first long journey of his life. He boarded a train to New York, and at Manhattan's bustling Grand Central Station switched to a train that was waiting to take him, as he later put it, into "the land of slaves." He was unsure what the days ahead would bring. But it was clear that he would never again live where the world intruded as gently as it did between the "quiet hills and golden river" of Great Barrington. ✦

3

THE MAKING
OF A
SCHOLAR

Du BOIS'S INITIAL REACTION to life at Fisk University was extremely positive. "I was thrilled to be for the first time among so many people of my own color," he noted in his autobiography. A modestly sized assemblage of educated and confident young men and women, the student body was by no means a representative group of southern blacks. Rather, it was, he said, "a microcosm of a world and a civilization in potentiality."

The 17-year-old Du Bois immediately launched what he called "my plan of study and accomplishment." He quickly became something of a campus celebrity. For one thing, the high quality of his public education allowed him to bypass his freshman year and enroll as a sophomore, a rare occurrence at Fisk. That he was from New England, and not the South, made him seem even more unusual to his fellow students and teachers. And then there was his tremendously impressive intellect, which he displayed in a variety of courses: Latin, Greek, French, calculus, chemistry, physics, and botany. When he became ill with typhoid fever a month after his arrival, the entire campus seemed to take a deep-seated interest in his welfare.

Du Bois made friends easily at Fisk. He edited the school newspaper, the *Fisk Herald*, attended dances in the homes of his classmates, and spent the rest of

Upon arriving at Fisk University in Nashville, Tennessee, in the fall of 1885, Du Bois "came in contact for the first time," he said, "with a sort of violence that I had never realized in New England." The South was "a region where the world was split into white and black halves, and where the darker half was held back by race prejudice and legal bonds, as well as by deep ignorance and dire poverty. . . . Into this world I leapt with enthusiasm."

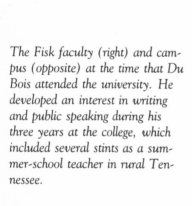

The Fisk faculty (right) and campus (opposite) at the time that Du Bois attended the university. He developed an interest in writing and public speaking during his three years at the college, which included several stints as a summer-school teacher in rural Tennessee.

his time continuing "to arrange and build my program for freedom and progress among Negroes." He found the Fisk campus, which he termed "nicely situated," to be a haven for blacks.

The surrounding area, however, left Du Bois exposed to the brutality of racial prejudice. Eighteen sixty-eight—the year of his birth—was also, he liked to point out, the time in American history when southern blacks were first granted voting privileges. Three years after the Civil War ended, liberal members of the Republican party, known as the Radical Republicans, began to push through Reconstruction measures to help freed slaves win their civil rights.

But their victory, as it turned out, was short-lived. In 1883, the U.S. Supreme Court overturned the

Civil Rights Act of 1875, which had outlawed discrimination in public facilities. With this decision, the groundwork for the "separate but equal" doctrine was laid, and southern states introduced a number of laws and customs that sought to keep blacks "in their place."

The Ku Klux Klan and other white supremacist groups used violence and intimidation to deny blacks their rights. The tactics employed by many other white southerners may not have been as blatant, but they were just as malicious, and Du Bois felt their sting. One day on the streets of Nashville, he accidentally bumped into a white woman. Instinctively, he raised his hat in apology. But the woman was not pacified. Her furious response took Du Bois by surprise and left a very deep impression on him. "I only sensed scorn and hate; the kind of despising which a dog

might incur," he later wrote. "Thereafter . . . I avoided the necessity of showing them [whites] courtesy of any sort."

After Du Bois completed his first year at Fisk, he decided to spend his summer vacation as a teacher in a rural school so he could become better acquainted with the average southern black. He eventually made his way to an area near Alexandria, a small farming village in eastern Tennessee, where classes had been held only once in the last 20 years. Unlike the well-furnished public schools he had attended in New England, the schoolhouse where he worked as a teacher was a primitive, windowless log hut. Planks served as benches for the students. There were no desks and few books.

Du Bois did not have to look further than the classroom to see that the lives of his black pupils were blighted by poverty. Racism and persecution stood as barriers to their progress. A 20-year-old black named Josie was typical of his 30 or so students. "She seemed to be the center of the family; always busy at service, or at home," Du Bois recalled in his autobiography. "She had about her a certain fineness, the shadow of an unconscious moral heroism that would willingly give all of life to make life broader, deeper, and fuller for her and hers."

When Du Bois returned to the area surrounding Alexandria a decade later, Josie was dead, exhausted by poverty and the struggle to help support her family. "How many heartfuls of sorrow shall balance a bushel of wheat?" he asked in an essay entitled "On Progress." "All this life and love and strife and failure, is it the twilight of nightfall or the flush of some faint-dawning day?"

For Du Bois, teaching in the country clearly marked the beginning of a new dawn. His work with the rural poor inflamed his social conscience, and he returned to eastern Tennessee as an instructor the

following summer. Day by day, he grew ever more committed to trying to help his fellow blacks by lifting what he called "the Veil that hung between us and Opportunity."

Du Bois had developed a clear picture of southern black life by the time his third and final year at Fisk rolled around. He often discussed black rights in the *Fisk Herald*, to which he sent an "Open Letter to Southern People," and in the public speeches that he had begun to give. He was, he said, "determined to make a scientific conquest of my environment, which would render the emancipation of the Negro race easier and quicker." He noted in a *Fisk Herald* editorial that he was devoting himself "toward a life that shall be an honor to the Race."

Du Bois (second from left) at the age of 20, with fellow members of Fisk University's class of 1888. His excellent scholastic record at Fisk earned him a place at Harvard College in Cambridge, Massachusetts, the following year.

During the four years that Du Bois attended Harvard, philosopher and psychologist William James was one of the leading lights of the faculty. "Of all teachers," Du Bois maintained, "he was my closest friend."

Du Bois topped off his studies at Fisk by giving a commencement address on the German chancellor Otto Eduard Leopold von Bismarck. At his graduation ceremonies in June 1888, Du Bois acknowledged that the German leader had "created a nation out of a mass of bickering people. . . . This foreshadowed in my mind the kind of thing American Negroes must do, marching forth with strength and determination under trained leadership."

To realize his place as one of the leaders, Du Bois planned his future with the utmost care. He believed that acquiring the best possible education was the key to attaining this lofty position, and so he turned down a scholarship to Hartford Theological Seminary. He had come to believe "too little in Christian dogma to become a minister," he later remarked. Instead, he pursued his earlier goal of attending Harvard.

Fortunately for Du Bois, the Massachusetts school had just begun to broaden its admissions policy and to seek greater diversity among its student body. Four years after the college turned down his application for admission, it offered him a grant of $250—provided that he enroll as an undergraduate in the junior class. The school refused to recognize his degree from Fisk because its academic program did not measure up to Harvard's standards.

Du Bois spent the summer of 1888 in the Midwest, where he served as the business manager for his friends in the Fisk Glee Club. An accomplished organizer and planner, he booked concert dates for the singing group. He also worked as a waiter in an attempt to supplement his scholarship money. When he arrived at Harvard that September, he took a cheap room off campus and set about establishing himself as one of the top students in his class of 300.

Harvard boasted an outstanding faculty that included the influential philosopher and psychologist William James, who became, Du Bois later claimed, "my friend and guide to clear thinking." Science, history, economics, and sociology were among the courses Du Bois took during his two years as a Harvard undergraduate. His chief subject of study was philosophy, a field in which he hoped one day to make a career.

The Harvard faculty quickly recognized Du Bois's interest in learning. Among his more notable scholastic accomplishments was winning a Matthews Scholarship in 1889. The following year, he garnered another award, taking second place in the Boylston Prize for oratory.

While Du Bois was being embraced as a brilliant black scholar by his professors, he chose to isolate himself from his many white peers at Harvard. He joined the Philosophical Club and Foxcraft, a university dining club. For the most part, though, he adopted a program of racial segregation. He purposely declined friendships with whites, he said, so he would be "encased in a completely colored world." He reasoned that he was preparing to enter one kind of society while the white students at Harvard were readying themselves for another, and he might as well brace himself for the days ahead by befriending blacks only.

Du Bois was also "desperately afraid," he said, "of intruding where I was not wanted." At Harvard, one of the few organizations he tried to join was the glee club. He had always taken great pleasure in singing; indeed, he had been a member of the choral society at Fisk. Yet his application to the Harvard Glee Club was turned down. "I ought to have known," he said later, "that Harvard could not afford to have a Negro on its Glee Club traveling about the country." He received some satisfaction when one of his teachers expelled a southern student from class because he objected to sitting next to Du Bois.

Du Bois often expressed his increasing dissatisfaction with America's racial policies in his classroom papers, several of which were published in the Boston

Courant, a small black weekly. Even so, he was not content with his writing ability and made a point of taking an English composition course to refine his grammar and style. "I believe, foolishly perhaps, but sincerely," he wrote in October 1890, "that I have something to say to the world, and I have taken English 12 in order to say it well."

Off campus, Du Bois led an active life. By studying intensively during the daytime, he was free at night to attend local black gatherings and help launch a production of Aristophanes' *The Birds* in a black Boston church. "I tried to take culture out into the colored community of Boston," he said. At a black protest rally, Du Bois met Maud Cuney, who was attending the New England Conservatory of Music. They soon fell in love and became engaged, although they never married.

In June 1890, Du Bois graduated with honors in philosophy. He was one of six students asked to speak at his undergraduate commencement, and he pointedly decided to make the subject of his address a champion of slavery: Jefferson Davis, whose military campaigns in the Black Hawk War in the 1830s and the Mexican War in the 1840s had been instrumental in his becoming the first—and only—president of the Confederate States of America.

Du Bois's speech, "Jefferson Davis as a Representative of Civilization," was as impassioned as it was caustic. Davis, he said, satisfied the nation's hunger for an individualist who was also an oppressor. Du Bois called the southern leader a "peculiar champion of a people fighting to be free in order that another people should not be free." Like all "strong men," he sought "the advance of a part of the world at the expense of the whole. . . . It has thus happened that advance in civilization has always been handicapped by shortsighted national selfishness."

The speech received an overwhelming response. "Du Bois handled his difficult and hazardous subject

A photograph of Du Bois taken from Harvard's class of 1890 album. Although he distinguished himself as one of the college's top students, he felt separated from the predominantly white student body and was quick to claim, "I was in Harvard, but not of it."

with absolute good taste, great moderation, and almost contemptuous fairness," the *Nation* reported. "He is an excellent scholar in every way, and altogether the best black man that has come to Cambridge," added a Harvard professor.

The American Historical Association promptly invited Du Bois to deliver a speech at one of its meetings in Washington, D.C., in December of the following year. An early version of his doctoral thesis, the speech was praised as "thrilling" by the *New York Independent*. "As one looked at him," the newspaper said of Du Bois, "one could not help saying 'Let us not worry about the future of our country in the matter of race distinctions.' "

The Henry Bromfield Rogers Memorial Fellowship in Political Science enabled Du Bois to remain

Du Bois (front row, far right) was one of six undergraduates chosen by Harvard to deliver a commencement address at the graduation ceremonies for the class of 1890. Five years later, he became the first black to receive a doctorate from the university.

at Harvard from 1890 to 1892 as a graduate student. He anticipated receiving his doctorate a couple of years later, as soon as his dissertation, "The Suppression of the African Slave-Trade to the United States of America, 1638–1870," was completed. Therefore, he had to prepare for the day when his two-year fellowship came to an end.

In late 1890, Du Bois applied for a grant from the John F. Slater Fund for Negro Education, a philanthropic organization established by a wealthy Connecticut textile manufacturer. Du Bois was determined "to become a recognized American scholar," and he believed that the best way to make that happen was by rounding off his education at a foreign university. It was the general view in the late 19th century that several universities in Germany offered the most rigorous academic program available. Du Bois set his sights accordingly.

Former U.S. president Rutherford B. Hayes chaired the Slater Fund. "If there is any young colored man in the South whom we find to have a talent for art or literature or any special aptitude for study," he reportedly said, "we are willing to give him money from the education funds to send him to Europe or give him advanced education." Du Bois certainly fit the bill. Buoyed by an outstanding record of intellectual accomplishments, he wrote directly to Hayes in November 1890. When this letter went unanswered, Du Bois sent off two more applications to the former president. Finally, in May 1891, Hayes responded. "The plan had been given up," the 23-year-old graduate student was told.

"I am perfectly capable of fighting alone for an education if the trustees do not see fit to help me," Du Bois wrote back angrily to Hayes. "On the other hand the injury you have—unwittingly I trust—done the race I represent, and am not ashamed of, is almost irreparable. . . . When now finally you receive three or four applications for the fulfillment of that offer, the offer is suddenly withdrawn, while the impression still remains." He went on to say, "I think you owe an apology to the Negro people. We are ready to furnish competent men. . . . But we can't educate ourselves on nothing."

Hayes promised to discuss the matter with the Slater fund's board of trustees at a future meeting. In the meantime, Du Bois mailed recommendations from his former teachers to Hayes, and his perseverance ultimately paid off. In April 1892, shortly before his Rogers fellowship was about to end, he received word that the board of the Slater fund was allotting him $750 to study abroad for a year. Only half of the amount was a gift, however. He had to repay the other half, with interest.

Du Bois arrived in Europe on August 1, 1892, after crossing the Atlantic on a Dutch steamer. "It is not real; I must be dreaming!" he constantly repeated to himself during the two-week voyage. He awoke from his reverie, however, as soon as he set foot on shore at Rotterdam, a port city in the Netherlands. He had two months before school started at Friedrich Wilhelm University in Berlin, and he wanted to see as much of the Continent as he could in the interim.

Du Bois's view of the relationship between blacks and whites underwent a noteworthy change during his European travels. "On mountain and valley, in home and school, I met men and women as I have never met them before," he wrote in his autobiography. "Slowly they became, not white folks, but folks." They treated him like the interesting, well-educated young man he was—not, he said, "as a curiosity, or something sub-human."

At Harvard, Du Bois had learned to accept the inevitability of racial separation. But the people whom he met in Europe caused him to rethink his views on racism altogether and to see prejudice and bigotry under a new light. He wrote, "I felt myself standing, not against the world, but simply against American narrowness and color prejudice, with the greater, finer world at my back urging me on."

Du Bois spent part of the summer in the German town of Eisenach. There he became enamored of Dora Marbach, an attractive young Dutch woman with black hair and blue eyes. She was just as captivated by the dark American and told Du Bois that she would like to marry him "at once." Although they never did wed—trying to endure an interracial marriage in America was not a pleasant prospect for Du Bois—their romance clearly left its mark on the black scholar. "I became more human; learned the place in life of 'Wine, Women, and Song,' " he later

"Had it not been for the race problem early thrust upon me and enveloping me," Du Bois wrote in his autobiography, "I should have probably been an unquestioning worshipper at the shrine of the established social order and of the economic development into which I was born. But just that part of this order which seemed to most of my fellows nearest perfection, seemed to me most inequitable and wrong; and starting from that critique, I gradually, as the years went by, found other things to question in my environment."

acknowledged. "I ceased to hate or suspect people simply because they belonged to one race or color."

That October, Du Bois began his studies in Berlin, the capital of the German empire. At the university, he took courses in economics, politics, and history. He supplemented his intensive classroom learning by exploring the lively city that lay beyond the school's walls.

"My attention from the first," Du Bois said, "was focused on democracy and democratic development; and upon the problem of the admission of my people into the freedom of democracy." In Berlin, he met students from all around the globe and listened carefully as they explained their world views. He attended meetings of Germany's Socialist party and discovered as he traveled during school vacations that oppression was not unique to the United States. He witnessed national rivalries, the incredible poverty of the serfs of eastern Europe (whose condition he considered worse than that of southern blacks), and racial antagonism (especially German anti-Semitism, with its pronounced discrimination against Jews) that was, he said, "only too familiar."

Du Bois also noted how the European colonial powers exploited the people of Africa. In his mind, the destinies of black Americans and Africans—both of whom suffered under imperialism—were connected. He wrote on his 25th birthday that he intended to "work for the rise of the Negro people, taking for granted that their best development means the best development of the world."

In mid-1893, the Slater fund renewed Du Bois's fellowship for one more year of study abroad. He remained at the university in Berlin, taking in the local culture and living "more or less regularly," as he later described it, with a young German woman for about a year. Their relationship ended for much the same reason that he had broken up with Dora Marbach: He was unwilling to suffer the consequences of an interracial marriage.

Du Bois's fellowship ran out just as he was completing his third semester at the German university. Doctoral candidates were supposed to attend classes for five semesters before they received their degree, and when the director of the Slater fund informed Du Bois in the spring of 1894 that his grant was not being renewed for the coming school year, he packed up his bags, dejected that he had to return home minus the prized doctorate.

Even without an official piece of paper to herald his efforts, Du Bois was ready to claim that his two years at Friedrich Wilhelm University had put the finishing touches on his formal education. "The years of preparation were over and life was to begin," he remarked. After a brief foray in Paris, he crossed over to England and booked his passage back to the United States.

As Du Bois boarded the SS *Chester* in June 1894, it was clear from his appearance that his personal habits as well as his thinking had been deeply influenced by his experiences in the Old World. Like most European gentlemen, he wore a high silk hat and white gloves and carried a cane. His beard and mustache were trimmed in the style of the German emperor, Wilhelm II. Even his brusque manner of speech had a Germanic flavor. "I gained a respect for manners," he offered as an explanation of his newly adopted customs.

A highly polished, self-made scholar, Du Bois stood on the deck of the ocean liner nine days later as it approached New York harbor. The first thing he saw of his native land was the Statue of Liberty, then just 10 years old, holding its torch aloft like a beacon of hope. For many, the massive sculpture was a symbol of freedom. But a little French girl who stood near Du Bois seemed to know better. She pointed out that the statue had its back turned toward America.

He was home. ❧

4

BEHIND
THE VEIL

◄○►

THE RACIAL CLIMATE in the United States had deteriorated during the two years that Du Bois was overseas, with the biggest shift naturally taking place in the South, where about 90 percent of the country's black population lived. In 1892, a nationwide economic depression caused agricultural prices to fall sharply. Southern sharecroppers were hit especially hard by the declining economy. Most of the region's farmers depended on a single cash crop—cotton—for their living, and having to sell their harvest at extremely low prices caused many of the farms to fail completely. Immediately thereafter, out-of-work white sharecroppers began to vie for the menial jobs that were normally held by blacks. Racial tensions started to mount, with the confrontations becoming increasingly hostile.

As the depression continued, black sharecroppers became the target of white terrorists. Following the Civil War, millions of freed slaves had rented parcels of land and took up tenant farming. Less than 30 years later, with the economy in turmoil and most farmers desperate to provide for their families, bands of white farmers decided to take matters into their own hands and drive blacks off desirable tracts of land.

The conservative white leaders who came into political power in the South, such as Pitchfork Ben Tillman, the governor of South Carolina, went a step further. They wanted to return blacks to slavelike

Du Bois returned to America in 1894 after studying at the University of Berlin for two years. He said, "It was a disturbed world in which I landed; 1892 saw the high tide of lynching in the United States, 235 untried Negroes being slaughtered in that one year."

conditions and worked to disfranchise black voters; they encouraged a segregated society that sought to keep blacks at the lowest possible social level; they even went so far as to encourage lynchings in an attempt to intimidate blacks into total subservience to white authority. In the 1890s, a black was lynched every three days—the highest rate in American history, and a murderous amount by any stretch of the imagination.

After mixing freely with whites in Europe, Du Bois was rudely reawakened by the treatment of blacks in the United States. When the SS *Chester* docked in New York, he returned at once to Great Barrington and began hunting for a job that would help him become "a leader of my people." Feeling that he was best qualified to teach, he mailed off letters to black colleges across the country, including Fisk University, Hampton Institute in Virginia, Howard University in Washington, D.C., and Tuskegee Institute in Alabama. "I was not exacting or hard to please," he recalled in his autobiography. "I just got down on my knees and begged for work, anything and anywhere."

In mid-August, Wilberforce University in Ohio offered the 26-year-old Du Bois a position to teach Latin and Greek. Although the classics was not his chief area of expertise, he needed a job and accepted the post. His salary was set at a modest $800 a year.

Du Bois arrived at Wilberforce with great expectations. Admittedly "cocky and self-satisfied," he planned to offer a class in sociology—the study of society, which was then in its infancy as an academic discipline—to complement his teaching of Latin and Greek. "I conceived the idea of applying philosophy to an historical interpetation of race relations," he explained. The school refused to let him go ahead with his plans, however, and he wound up teaching courses in German and English along with the classics.

Du Bois worked hard at Wilberforce. He had high aspirations for his students and demanded nearly as much from them as he did from himself. Yet he failed to become one of the most popular professors on the Ohio campus. Although his willingness to work long hours and his excellent educational background stood him in good stead, his bearing and outspoken nature sometimes caused problems. He arrived at his classes and faculty meetings wearing a European silk hat and gloves and carrying a cane—a style of dress that looked out of place in Middle America. He was dapper and sharp tongued and independent minded— traits that did not go over well at a school run by the staid African Methodist Episcopal church.

On one occasion, Du Bois created a furor while visiting a student prayer meeting. As he entered the room, the group's leader told the other students that Du Bois would guide them in prayer. "No, he won't," the professor responded, unwilling to accept the impromptu religious practices that were a regular part of campus life. His refusal angered the members of the school board and almost cost him his job.

Du Bois's religious convictions ultimately isolated him from the rest of the community, yet he managed

Du Bois's first teaching post upon his return to the United States in 1894 was at Wilberforce University in Wilberforce, Ohio. "Into this institution I landed with the cane and gloves of my German student days; with my rather inflated ideas of what a university ought to be," he said.

to put the time he had to himself to good use. During his first year at Wilberforce, he made a habit of staying in his room and working on "The Suppression of the African Slave-Trade to the United States of America, 1638–1870," the doctoral dissertation he had begun at Harvard University. In 1895, the dissertation was accepted by Harvard, which awarded him a Ph.D. in philosophy. The text was published one year later, in October 1896, as the first volume in a series of historical studies issued by the university. All told, the book received some excellent reviews, especially from the *Nation*, which called it "the authoritative work on the subject."

By the time his first book was published, Du Bois had agreed to leave Wilberforce and had accepted a one-year offer to teach at the University of Pennsylvania. In addition to serving as an assistant instructor in sociology at the Philadelphia-based school, he was asked to perform extensive social research on a local black neighborhood. In 1896, the City of Brotherly Love was facing grave racial problems, with one of its black ghettos, the Seventh Ward, fast becoming a notorious center for crime, violence, and poverty. Civic leaders were particularly interested in understanding the factors that led to these developments and wanted Du Bois to investigate the social structure of the black community. "The opportunity opened at the University of Pennsylvania seemed just what I wanted," he said.

Accompanying Du Bois to Philadelphia was his new bride, Nina Gomer. They had met earlier in the year at Wilberforce, where she had been a student. "A slip of a girl, beautifully dark-eyed," according to Du Bois, she came from the sedate community of Cedar Rapids, Iowa, a far cry from the dirty, crime-ridden streets of Philadelphia.

The newlyweds rented a small apartment in the heart of the Seventh Ward to facilitate Du Bois's investigation of the surrounding area. "Murder sat on our doorsteps" was the way he described the world outside his home. Yet he set about his research with enormous enthusiasm. "The Negro problem," he maintained, "was in my mind a matter of systematic investigation and intelligent understanding. The world was thinking wrong about race, because it did not know. . . . The cure for it was knowledge based on scientific investigation."

Du Bois worked entirely by himself on the research project. He began by interviewing every household in the district, block by block. Within a few months, he had questioned more than 5,000 people about every aspect of their life: What is your occupation? What kinds of jobs are you excluded from? Do any of your children go to school? Most of the blacks he interviewed resented being studied like some sort of exotic species, yet he persisted.

By the end of 1897, Du Bois had compiled a tremendous amount of information, piecing together two centuries' worth of Philadelphia history. The conclusions that he drew from his findings were published two years later under the title *The Philadelphia Negro: A Social Study*. Among Du Bois's most important assessments was that the city's blacks were "a symptom, not a cause; . . . a striving, palpitating group and not an inert, sick body of crime." They had few chances for advancement because whites denied them such rights as equal employment and fair housing.

But white society was not entirely to blame. The plight of Philadelphia's black poor was made even worse by other blacks. Du Bois's research showed that a basic class system existed in the black community, with middle-class blacks doing very little to improve the life of their lower-class brethren. Chief among the lapses of what he called the "black aristocracy" was its failure to create jobs for black workers. "The

In 1897, Atlanta University president Horace Bumstead hired Du Bois to teach history and economics at the school. Bumstead soon learned to appreciate "the stimulating personal influence of Doctor Du Bois upon our students. He had acquired his own education where the highest standards prevailed, and he would tolerate no lower ones in his own classrooms. Not only in study but also in conduct, he demanded of his pupils the best that was in them."

better classes of Negroes should recognize their duty toward the masses," he wrote in *The Philadelphia Negro*. He concluded that blacks would emerge from oppression only when strong leadership emerged to provide role models as well as a political voice.

The first sociological study of a black ghetto to be published in the United States, Du Bois's book was hailed by a number of scholarly journals, including the *Yale Review*, which called it "a credit to American scholarship and a distinct and valuable addition to the world's stock of knowledge." It remained just as highly regarded nearly 50 years later, when the noted Swedish sociologist and economist Gunnar Myrdal claimed that the study "best meets our requirements" for an examination of a black community. Yet this ground-breaking project was ultimately ignored by the University of Pennsylvania, which had commissioned the study. The school let Du Bois go as soon as his fieldwork was finished in 1897.

That same year, the 29-year-old scholar was appointed professor of history and economics at Atlanta University, a black school in Georgia. Horace Bumstead, the president of the school, had met Du Bois the year before, at an Alabama conference on the life of rural blacks. Bumstead knew of Du Bois's research and told him about his plans for holding a conference that would focus on the problems of black urban life. Du Bois was the ideal man for both jobs, Bumstead said in offering him the dual post of teacher and conference director.

In late 1897, Du Bois settled in the South for the second time. With him were his wife, Nina, and their newborn son, Burghardt Gomer, prompting Du Bois to approach his tenure at Atlanta University as a time of elation and hope. The high expectations of his students added wonderfully to the sense of excitement. "Not at Berlin . . . not at Harvard nor Yale," he wrote, "is there an air of higher resolve or more unfettered striving." He felt instantly at home in Atlanta and dropped most of the mannerisms that he had affected overseas. "I grew more broadly human," he said of his years at the university, "made my closest and most holy friendships." His deepest friendship was with John Hope, a fellow teacher who later became president of the school.

The field of black sociology was established under Du Bois's stewardship at Atlanta University. In May 1898, he launched a series of annual conferences on the problems plaguing black Americans. Two years earlier, the school had sponsored a conference that bore little resemblance to the ambitious program Du Bois put into operation. Much like the annual conferences held at Tuskegee Institute, Hampton Institute, and other southern black schools, the Atlanta Conference of 1896 had been an inspirational meeting aimed at encouraging specific types of social work for blacks. Du Bois, however, was not interested in reform efforts that followed preconceived notions. The main purpose of his Atlanta conference was to gather concrete information and have it become "a basis for further study," he said, "rather than an organ of social reform."

Du Bois initially planned on researching 10 particular subjects—among them religion, politics, education, and population—over a 10-year period. After a decade, research would start again on the same topics—broadening and intensifying the investigation as needed, decade after decade—until an encyclopedia of black American life was created, representing 100 years of study. "Through this laboratory experiment I hoped to make the laws of social living clearer, surer, and more definite," he said.

The enterprise continued with Du Bois at the helm for 20 years and was instrumental in transforming him into a nationally known black scholar. After each conference, Atlanta University published Du

While serving as a professor at Atlanta University, Du Bois organized a series of annual conferences that examined the problems facing black Americans. "The ultimate evil was ignorance and its child, stupidity," he said. "The cure for it was knowledge based on study."

Bois's studies. These annual publications—then the only available scientific studies on black life in the entire world—were widely consulted by political leaders and scholars. "I have just looked through the last installment of your studies on the American Negro," William James wrote to Du Bois in 1907. "It is splendid scientific work." Countless other men of learning were quick to agree, especially in an age when virtually all other published material about black Americans was racist propaganda.

Du Bois did his best to counter these racist views. He responded to the Georgia legislature's attempt to disfranchise black voters by publishing an essay defending black rights. He testified before an industrial commission held by the House of Representatives in Washington, D.C., and called for improvement in the education of southern blacks. He spoke out against lynchings and Jim Crow laws—segregation laws sanctioned by the U.S. Supreme Court's 1896 ruling that separate accommodations for blacks and whites were legal as long as the separate facilities were roughly equal in quality. These laws invariably permitted state and city governments to treat black Americans as second-class citizens.

As Du Bois watched racism and political oppression increase in the United States, he seemed to be caught between two movements: blacks who lobbied for racial solidarity and decried integration, and blacks who denounced racial separation and called for full assimilation into white society. But Du Bois, whose scientific method called for him to base his conclusions on the information at hand, did not join either faction. Instead, he adopted a position on race relations that took into account his being both black *and* American.

At the first convention of the American Negro Academy in 1897, Du Bois stated to the other members of this small organization of black scholars, "We are Americans, not only by birth and citizenship, but by our political ideals, our language, our religion. Farther than that, our Americanism does not go. At that point, we are Negroes, members of a vast historic race . . . the first fruits of this new nation." He urged his fellow blacks to retain their cultural identity and to foster black art and literature. Instead of practicing individual self-reliance, they should cooperate economically with one another and "buy black." Above all, they should try to do things for themselves rather than wait for civil rights bills to be passed on their behalf.

In the midst of his call for social change, Du Bois suffered a tragic loss. His son, Burghardt, died in the spring of 1899 after succumbing to sewage pollution in the Atlanta water supply. "The child's death tore our lives in two," Du Bois said of Nina and himself. "I threw myself more completely into my work, while most reason for living left the soul of my wife."

Among the many projects Du Bois took on was an exhibit on black American life slated to be shown at the Paris Exposition, a huge world's fair held in 1900. That spring, shortly before the birth of his daughter, Yolande, he traveled to France to set up

Du Bois with his first wife, Nina, and their son, Burghardt, in a photograph (probably taken in 1899, just before the boy died) that Du Bois carried around for many years. The couple's only other child, a daughter, Yolande (opposite), was born 16 months after Burghardt's death.

the display and was duly rewarded for his efforts. The exhibit, which occupied a small room, won a grand prize and added to his growing international reputation as a scholar and a champion of black America.

Toward the end of his second trip to Europe, Du Bois met with a group of 32 men and women who shared an even larger interest: advancing the civil rights of Africans and their descendants around the globe. Convening in London, England, they formed the Pan-African Association and named Du Bois the organization's chairman. He was the obvious choice for the post. One of the first thinkers to promote worldwide unity among blacks as a means for the African colonies to gain their independence from the industrial nations of Europe, he was regarded by his peers as the meeting's most distinguished delegate. Although the association folded two years later, Du Bois remained devoted to the cause of a free Africa, and he became known in the ensuing years as the father of Pan-Africanism.

Back in the United States, Du Bois made sure to air his views on Pan-Africanism and other political and social issues to the general public. In essays written for the *Atlantic Monthly*, the *New York Times Magazine*, and other periodicals, he discussed such topics as "Strivings of the Negro People," "The Freedmen's Bureau," and "The Black North." In 1902, a Chicago publisher approached Du Bois and offered to bring out a collection of these essays. They were published one year later under the title *The Souls of Black Folk: Essays and Sketches*, and the book became Du Bois's first literary success.

The 14 essays that make up *The Souls of Black Folk* had little in common with Du Bois's scholarly tracts. Written with undeniable power and grace, each of these pieces came across as an impassioned quest for racial identity. Indeed, these urgent essays still strike a deep chord when they are read today.

The book's clever title suggests the probing nature of the essays. Du Bois picked the word *souls* to indicate the divided nature of black Americans: Being black as well as American, they seemed to have two identities. The use of the double-edged *souls* stood in sharp contrast to the term *folk*, which emphasized that blacks nevertheless had an identity that separated them from other Americans.

"After the Egyptian and Indian, the Greek and Roman, the Teuton and Mongolian," Du Bois wrote in the first chapter of *The Souls of Black Folk*, "the Negro is a sort of Seventh son, born with a veil, and gifted with second sight in this American world." The "veil" was the fabric of racism that kept blacks concealed from whites, and it also kept blacks from seeing themselves clearly. "It is a peculiar sensation, this double-consciousness, this sense of always looking at oneself through the eyes of others, of measuring one's soul by the tape of the world that looks on in amused contempt and pity," Du Bois acknowledged.

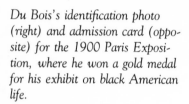

Du Bois's identification photo (right) and admission card (opposite) for the 1900 Paris Exposition, where he won a gold medal for his exhibit on black American life.

"One ever feels his twoness—an American, a Negro; two souls, two thoughts, two unreconciled strivings, two warring ideals in one dark body, whose dogged strength alone keeps it from being torn asunder."

The book contained essays on a wide range of topics, including religion, Negro spirituals, and slave life. Yet they all touched on one major point. "The problem of the twentieth century is the problem of the color line," Du Bois wrote in "Of the Dawn of Freedom," the volume's second essay. It was to become one of his bluntest and best-known statements.

"Of Mr. Booker T. Washington and Others," which Du Bois wrote specially for the collection, was the essay that gained the most attention. Du Bois later described this piece as "a frank evaluation" of the one black spokesman who had gained the trust of white leaders. Indeed, Washington's actions had an impact on every black in America, above all Du Bois, whom the Tuskegee principal came to view as his chief rival.

Washington's background could not have been more different from Du Bois's. Washington, who was born a slave in Virginia before the Civil War, never had the advantages of an early education. As a boy, he had been sent to the salt mines, where he had managed to teach himself to read. He then found work as a janitor at Hampton Normal and Agricultural Institute, a black college in Virginia, where he also took several classes and eventually became a teacher.

Unlike Washington, most former slaves became sharecroppers. Poor agricultural methods, fluctuating prices, and an overreliance on cotton as a cash crop were just a few of the problems that left black sharecroppers constantly in debt and made it seem as though they had simply exchanged physical slavery for financial slavery. Washington was sensitive to the economic needs of these former slaves and wanted to teach them how to make their land more productive. Accordingly, he developed a philosophy of education that centered on the need for job training.

The state of Alabama gave Washington the opportunity to develop a program of industrial training. Because it did not wish to integrate any of its schools, the state decided to create a black institute of higher education and asked Washington to head the new facility. Alabama then showed its true commitment

to higher education for blacks by denying Washington every resource he needed to create the school other than the land on which it was to stand.

Tuskegee Normal and Industrial Institute held its first classes inside a church in 1881. With the help of his fellow teachers and students, Washington soon built a more permanent school, brick by brick, in the town of Tuskegee. He courted white philanthropists, such as steel baron Andrew Carnegie, for the funds that supported the school, and he assembled a top-flight faculty by luring the scientist George Washington Carver and other black scholars to rural Alabama. By the turn of the century, Tuskegee had become one of the nation's most important black institutions, with an enrollment of nearly 1,000 students and a teaching staff of more than 100. And Washington had become the country's leading black spokesman.

The key moment in Washington's rise to national prominence took place in 1895, at the Cotton States and International Exposition in Atlanta. Speaking before an audience of blacks and whites, he called for blacks to put aside their aspirations for political and social equality. Instead, he said, they should take part in the South's economic development and focus on improving their industrial skills before demanding a higher place in American society.

Washington promised the whites in the crowd that blacks, in building their own industries, would loyally and unresentfully participate in revitalizing the South. "The wisest among my race understand that the agitation of questions of social equality is the extremest folly," he said. Social and political equality would follow once blacks had made a substantial economic contribution to the nation.

In effect, Washington was saying that blacks were willing to accept racial segregation if whites agreed to let them have their own institutions. Du Bois dubbed the speech the "Atlanta Compromise" and saw others embrace it with great enthusiasm. U.S. president Grover Cleveland, for one, said that the speech offered "new hope" for black Americans, and most of the country's policymakers seemed to agree. Before long, Washington was being consulted on every aspect of the "Negro problem."

A number of influential blacks, including journalists Ida Wells-Barnett and William Monroe Trotter, disagreed vigorously with Washington's sentiments and felt that his views were a betrayal of their civil rights. Du Bois, however, was initially sympathetic to Washington. *The Philadelphia Negro* had also promoted the virtues of thrift and self-reliance as solutions to the problems faced by blacks. Moreover, Washington was proud of his race and was

Du Bois with Atlanta University president Horace Bumstead. Du Bois said prior to arriving at the school, "History and the other social sciences were to be my weapons, to be sharpened and applied by research and writing."

interested in black unity. Du Bois wrote that the Atlanta Compromise "might be the basis of a real settlement between whites and blacks in the South."

But by the early 1900s, racial relations in the United States had continued to worsen, and a growing number of blacks believed that Washington had contributed significantly to this downward turn of events. Blacks faced stiffer segregation laws and enjoyed fewer voting privileges than they had in decades. And Washington's thinking had grown more rigid in the process. He failed to support black voting rights and lobbied for agricultural and industrial training at the expense of higher learning—an attitude that clearly irritated Du Bois and the growing, younger class of educated blacks.

To make matters worse, Washington took advantage of his position of power to create an influential network that became known as the Tuskegee machine. This widespread group of supporters, which included congressmen, philanthropists, and educators, spread his doctrines, promoted those who thought as he did, and sabotaged the careers of his opponents. "After a time," Du Bois noted, "almost no Negro institution could collect funds without the recommendation or acquiescence of Mr. Washington."

Du Bois had been in contact with the nation's leading black spokesman as early as 1894, when the job-hunting scholar had declined a spot on the Tuskegee faculty because he had just promised to teach at Wilberforce. Eight years later, he again came close to working at Tuskegee, when the industrialist William Henry Baldwin, the school's most powerful trustee, recruited him for a position at the institute. Du Bois sat through two interviews with Washington in New York but did not pursue the job any further because the exact nature of the post was never defined.

While serving as principal of Tuskegee Institute, the nation's leading black industrial school, Booker T. Washington (front row, center) became head of the "Tuskegee machine," an influential group of politicians, industrialists, and educators that sought to advance Washington's views on black affairs. By the early 1900s, most members of this powerful network—including the steel baron Andrew Carnegie (second from right)—regarded the outspoken Du Bois as one of their chief opponents.

That same year, Du Bois was all set to edit a national journal focusing on black issues. But when he indicated to the periodical's financial backers, who were Washington supporters, that his editor's pen would not necessarily follow the principles of Washington's philosophy, they abruptly canceled the project. More and more, it seemed to Du Bois, the Tuskegee machine was looking to silence its critics without regard to their right to free speech.

A resentful Du Bois wrote "Of Mr. Booker T. Washington and Others" in an attempt to stop the steamroller effect of the Tuskegee machine. The essay supported Washington's encouragement of thrift and economic growth but went on to criticize other aspects of the Tuskegee philosophy. Du Bois argued that Washington's program was "a gospel of work and money" that denied "the higher aims of life" and "tended to shift the burden of the Negro problem to the Negro's shoulders." Moreover, the constant promotion of industrial training jeopardized the development of black higher education and thus prevented black leadership from emerging.

Du Bois lashed out at Washington's "old attitude of adjustment and submission" and proposed an alternative. He said that the educated black elite, the small percentage of black intellectuals whom he referred to as "the Talented Tenth," should provide the strong leadership that the nation's blacks so desperately needed. "The Negro race, like all races, is going to be saved by its exceptional men," he wrote. Rather than attempt to secure good jobs and generate wealth (as Washington wanted them to), Du Bois insisted that middle-class blacks use their advanced knowledge of modern culture to lead the struggle for black rights. The Talented Tenth theory, which grew out of the conclusions Du Bois had reached in *The Philadelphia Negro*, seemed to him the only way to supplant white—and thus Washington's—leadership.

The Tuskegee machine immediately went into action to discredit Du Bois's claims against Washington. Black newspapers attacked the 35-year-old professor for his "petty annoyances." One periodical even asked Atlanta University president Horace Bumstead to silence the "ill-advised criticisms of the learned Doctor."

The attacks on Du Bois continued through the spring of 1903 and reached a climax in July, when Washington gave an address before 2,000 listeners in Boston. William Monroe Trotter, one of Du Bois's Harvard classmates and cofounder of a liberal black newspaper, the *Boston Guardian*, disrupted the speech and was subsequently arrested and imprisoned. When Du Bois stated that Trotter's monthlong jail term was far too heavy a sentence, Washington concluded incorrectly that Du Bois had been behind the distur-

William Monroe Trotter was cofounder and editor of the Boston Guardian, *a black weekly newspaper that savagely attacked the accommodationist policies of Booker T. Washington. Du Bois worked closely with Trotter on several occasions.*

bance and stepped up his campaign of retaliation. Washington told the white philanthropists who supported Atlanta University that they should stop funding the college.

Despite these shows of power, which further antagonized Du Bois and other liberal blacks, Washington hoped to resolve his differences with his opponents. Accordingly, in January 1904 he sponsored a huge conference of prominent black leaders in New York's Carnegie Hall that was to be, he said, "the most important, serious and far-reaching in the history of our people." Yet the three-day conference proved to be a one-sided affair. Washington and his followers—including Andrew Carnegie, William Henry Baldwin, and Oswald Garrison Villard, editor of the *New York Evening Post* and grandson of the noted abolitionist William Lloyd Garrison—seized control of the meetings and garnered most of the spots on the Committee of Twelve, an executive group that was to act as a national steering committee for blacks.

Du Bois tried to work with the committee but found his path continually blocked by Washington's supporters. In April 1904, he finally gave up and attacked Washington in print. Du Bois charged that Washington had bribed a number of black newspapers to make them support the Tuskegee philosophy. America's leading black spokesman, Du Bois claimed, "was seeking not the welfare of the Negro race but personal power."

Du Bois's attacks on Washington were accurate, yet they did little to displace the Tuskegee principal from his position of influence. To accomplish that, Du Bois realized, he would have to take a completely different tack. He had been suggesting for years that new black leadership was needed. Now it was up to him to step forward and see that it emerged. ◆

5

"A CRITICAL TIME"

·❧·

IN JUNE 1905, Du Bois boldly issued a call "for organized determination and aggressive action on the part of men who believe in Negro freedom and growth." The appeal was not very far-reaching, but it was not meant to be. Du Bois limited the call to a select group of influential blacks, asking them to convene the following month in a remote location—Fort Erie, Ontario, close to Niagara Falls—to discuss the current state of black affairs.

Booker T. Washington soon found out about the Canadian conference and made certain that the black press gave it little coverage. He also pressured a number of blacks into avoiding the summit. Still, 29 men and women from 14 states answered Du Bois's call and gave rise to an organization known as the Niagara Movement. Among the objectives that they established at their first conference were "freedom of speech and criticism," "the abolition of all caste distinctions based simply on race or color," and "the recognition of the principle of human brotherhood."

Acknowledging that the infant organization was extremely small in comparison with the powerful Tuskegee machine, Du Bois launched a liberal journal, the *Moon: Illustrated Weekly*, to publicize the Niagara Movement's views. The first issue, published in December 1905, failed to reach a large audience, and the magazine ground to a halt a half year later. Du Bois then started up another journal, *Horizon*, which was slightly more successful. It lasted for three years.

In response to Booker T. Washington's accommodationist policies, Du Bois (middle row, second from right) secretly organized the Niagara Movement, which held its first meeting near Niagara Falls in July 1905. The first public meeting of the movement took place the following year, at Harpers Ferry, West Virginia, with Du Bois proclaiming in an "Address to the Country": "We want our children trained as intelligent human beings should be and we will fight for all time against any proposal to educate black boys and girls simply as servants and underlings, or simply for the use of other people."

Du Bois supplemented his editorial work by writing articles on black issues for some of the nation's leading magazines, including the *Nation, Collier's,* and *Dial.* He tackled lengthier projects as well. In 1903, he published a *Bibliography of Negro Folk Songs,* a compilation of black spirituals. The following year, he started work on a novel, *The Quest of the Silver Fleece.* And in 1905 he began writing *John Brown,* a biography, published four years later, of the white abolitionist who led a slave uprising at Harpers Ferry, West Virginia, in 1859.

"My career as a scientist," Du Bois noted in his autobiography, "was to be swallowed up in my role as master of propaganda." Atlanta University's mounting financial worries did not make his situation any easier. Washington's continued opposition to Du Bois resulted in a decrease in funds coming into the school, which made it increasingly difficult for the Atlanta-based scholar to organize the university's annual conferences.

Yet Du Bois continued to criticize the Tuskegee philosophy, and Washington continued to attack the Niagara Movement. Despite the small size of the rival organization, Washington was disturbed by its existence and attempted to crush the movement in a variety of unscrupulous ways, including getting his supporters to infiltrate the Niagarites' second conference, held in 1906 at Harpers Ferry. By that time, the membership of the Niagara Movement had grown to 170 people, all of them obvious examples of Du Bois's Talented Tenth.

In the end, the battle between the Tuskegee machine and the Niagara Movement to gain the support of America's blacks proved to be a one-sided contest. Washington had few problems containing his opposition, and by 1908 various members of the Niagara group had started to jump ship and join other civil rights organizations, most notably the interracial

Constitution League. Du Bois accepted part of the blame. "I was no natural leader of men," he wrote in *Dusk of Dawn*. "I could not slap people on the back and make friends of strangers."

As the Niagara Movement began to wane, a rising tide of racial violence created a new set of problems for Washington. In August 1906, the nation's attention was captured by a race riot in Brownsville, Texas, which resulted in the dishonorable discharge of the black army troops stationed there. One month later, another attack on blacks occurred in Atlanta. The Tuskegee machine was predictably ineffective in combating the forces of white racism.

If there was any further need to dramatize the necessity of having a strong organization to lobby for and protect black rights, it came in 1908, when the white journalist William English Walling witnessed

Du Bois and William Monroe Trotter (front row) with participants in the Niagara Movement's 1907 national conference, which was held in Boston, Massachusetts. "We will not be satisfied to take one jot or tittle [sic] less than our full manhood rights," the movement stated. "We claim for ourselves every single right that belongs to a freeborn American, political, civil, and social; and until we get these rights we will never cease to protest and assail the ears of America."

In September 1908, journalist William English Walling wrote in an impassioned account of a Springfield, Illinois, race riot that a new organization was needed to fight for black rights. One year later, social worker Mary Ovington (opposite) helped coordinate a meeting of the National Negro Committee, an interracial group that evolved into the National Association for the Advancement of Colored People (NAACP).

an assault on blacks in Springfield, Illinois, the birth-place of "the Great Emancipator," Abraham Lincoln. Walling was so outraged by the riot that he challenged white liberals to take up the fight for racial justice. "We must come to treat the Negro on a plane of absolute political and social equality," he wrote in an essay, "or [white supremacists James] Vardaman and [Pitchfork Ben] Tillman will soon have trans-ferred the Race War to the North."

Walling's challenge was answered by 43-year-old Mary Ovington, a white social reformer. Du Bois had been in contact with her since 1904, when she had asked for his advice in undertaking a sociological study of black New Yorkers. They met the following year at the annual Atlanta Conference, and there-after her commitment to black civil rights never wa-vered. In response to Walling's essay, she organized— with the help of Walling and the social worker Dr. Henry Moskowitz—a conference on the status of blacks in the United States. Oswald Garrison Villard, a former Washington supporter, issued the call for a National Negro Committee for black advancement. Sixty people attended its first session, which was held on May 31, 1909, in New York.

Some of Washington's most ardent critics, es-pecially William Monroe Trotter, were suspicious of the aims of the white-dominated conference. But Du Bois refused to let slip away an opportunity to speak to a roomful of social activists, even if many of them were Washington backers. In his address to the as-sembly, he carefully outlined his objections to the Tuskegee philosophy and asserted the need for black equality. "I was more impressed with him than ever before," Villard noted afterward.

Du Bois was enthusiastic as well. He believed that the National Negro Committee marked "a new al-liance between social workers and reformers." A Committee of 40, a steering group that included Du

Bois, was formed to map out the workings of the association. Shortly thereafter, it established a permanent organization, the National Association for the Advancement of Colored People (NAACP).

The members of the NAACP elected their national officers at a conference in May 1910. Moorfield Storey, a prominent lawyer, was made president, Walling was named head of the executive committee, and Villard became disbursing treasurer. Du Bois was given the position of director of publicity and research—the only black to be offered a position on the new organization's board.

Three months later, Du Bois left Atlanta and moved with Nina and 10-year-old Yolande to New York City, where the NAACP had its headquarters. They stayed with one of his former students in Brooklyn. And each day Du Bois traveled to the NAACP office, located on Vesey Street in Manhattan.

Life in the thriving city was vastly different from the world Du Bois had experienced on the secluded campus of Atlanta University. Racial segregation was far less conspicuous in New York. "All the days of their lives they had heard about it," the poet Paul Laurence Dunbar said in describing how most black Americans regarded the nation's largest city, "and it seemed to them the center of all the glory, all the wealth, and all the freedom of the world."

New York was not quite the paradise many blacks made it out to be—racism was practiced there as much as in other northern centers—but the bustling city did have its attractions. Chief among them was Harlem, a northern district with plenty of affordable housing. In 1910, the same year that Du Bois arrived in New York, blacks began to move to Harlem in increasingly large numbers. By the end of the decade, they had managed to turn it into the largest and liveliest black community in the country, filling it with a variety of black institutions and organizations.

As NAACP director of publicity and research, Du Bois was anxious to make his mark on Harlem and other black communities. Stepping "out of my ivory tower of statistics and investigation," he later wrote in *Dusk of Dawn*, "I sought with bare hands to lift the earth and put it in the path in which I conceived it ought to go." His main project was establishing a monthly journal that would "set forth those facts and arguments which show the danger of race prejudice, particularly as manifested toward colored

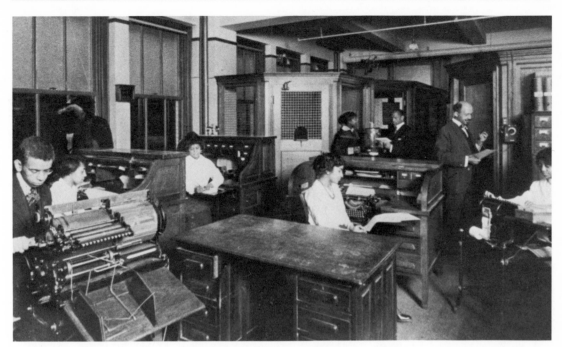

people," he explained in the first issue of the monthly, which he called the *Crisis*. "It takes its name from the fact that the editors believe that this is a critical time."

Du Bois outlined the journal's makeup in his very first editorial. "It will record important happenings and movements in the world which bear on the great problem of interracial relations," he wrote. It would also serve as a review of opinion and literature and feature an editorial page that would "stand for the rights of men."

An enthusiastic Du Bois ordered the printing of a thousand copies for the first issue, which he had ready by November 1910. It was sold by mail, in bookstores, and later at some newsstands. He figured that its only readers would be members of the Talented Tenth. But the *Crisis* appealed to a wider audience, from northern liberals to rural blacks in the South, and the circulation of subsequent issues increased dramatically. By the following year, 16,000

Du Bois in the New York office where he edited the NAACP's official publication, the Crisis. *When the association was first formed in 1909, he "carefully avoided the temptation of becoming its executive head," he said. "I still clung to my idea of investigation in lines which would temper and guide my exposition of a racial philosophy; and for that reason I determined from the beginning to make my work with the Association not that of executive secretary but editor of an official organ."*

copies were being printed, and within 10 years the circulation surged to 100,000.

NAACP board members noted how effectively the *Crisis* publicized the association's activities. With the growth of the journal came a significant rise in the organization's membership, and branch offices soon sprang up across the country. By the end of its first decade, the NAACP had approximately 90,000 members.

The militant tone of the *Crisis*, which was new for black journalism, was largely responsible for attracting so many readers. The monthly features were designed to interest a large readership as well. Each issue included brief biographies of prominent blacks, a column on recommended reading, and an educational and legal directory. Another regular feature was a list of the names and addresses of the NAACP leadership so readers knew where to reach the association.

The *Crisis* may have been the NAACP's official organ, but Du Bois controlled its contents and made certain that it reflected his own views. His ability to gain absolute authority over the journal was a startling accomplishment considering that the organization was ruled principally by whites and depended chiefly on white philanthropists for its funds. Yet it was difficult to argue with the success of his approach.

As each issue reached the public, it became more and more obvious that Du Bois had a remarkable ability for absorbing and commenting on all aspects of society. His articles and editorials covered a wide range of topics—among them politics, business, health, education, literature, and music. There was only one subject that did not receive the full brunt of his editor's pen. In keeping with the moderate feelings of the organization's board, the journal did not become an anti-Washington periodical.

Nevertheless, Washington made a number of attempts to silence the *Crisis*. He attacked the NAACP

THE CRISIS

A RECORD OF THE DARKER RACES

Volume One   NOVEMBER, 1910   Number One

Edited by W. E. BURGHARDT DU BOIS, with the co-operation of Oswald Garrison Villard, J. Max Barber, Charles Edward Russell, Kelly Miller, W. S. Braithwaite and M. D. Maclean.

CONTENTS

PUBLISHED MONTHLY BY THE

National Association for the Advancement of Colored People

AT TWENTY VESEY STREET   NEW YORK CITY

ONE DOLLAR A YEAR   TEN CENTS A COPY

The first issue of the Crisis, edited by Du Bois and published by the NAACP in November 1910. "The voice of protest of ten million Americans must never cease to assail the ears of their fellows, so long as America is unjust," he said.

whenever he had the chance and went so far as to encourage journalist T. Thomas Fortune to turn his *New York Age* into a rival black paper. "When we get done with Dr. Du Bois," Washington said, "I am sure that he will have some trouble in handing over leadership of the race to white men."

Washington, however, was the first one to fall. In March 1911, he went looking for a friend in a New York apartment building and accidently entered the residence of a white man named Henry Ulrich. Believing that Washington was there to burglarize his apartment, Ulrich grabbed a walking stick and beat the nation's most noted black. Washington responded to Ulrich's attack by filing an assault charge. Yet the Tuskegee principal was so evasive with his answers during the trial that a cloud of doubt settled over his integrity, and his political influence began to decline.

Under Du Bois's guidance, the Crisis *quickly gained a large audience. "I was an avid reader of the* Crisis, *from my earliest literate days," claimed Horace Mann Bond, a leading educator. "Through the* Crisis *Du Bois helped shape my inner world to a degree impossible to imagine in the world of contemporary children, and the flood of various mass media to which they are exposed. I remember the pleasant faces of brown and black children pictured in the magazine; I remember the photographs of decently garbed men and women of color, never seen elsewhere in the publications that came to our home."*

Things got worse for Washington the following year. Woodrow Wilson's election to the presidency in 1912 marked the first time in more than 15 years that the nation was headed by the Democratic rather than the Republican party, which ardently supported Washington's views. Many of the big wheels in the Tuskegee machine who had spent years attaining their political clout soon fell out of power.

By the time Washington died, on November 13, 1915, in Tuskegee, many of his supporters had joined the NAACP camp. Worsening racial conditions in the South, where segregation laws were being tightened and lynchings were still being practiced, prompted the realization that a bolder approach than the Tuskegee philosophy was desperately needed. "He was the greatest Negro leader since [the abolitionist] Frederick Douglass," Du Bois wrote in the *Crisis* one month after Washington's death. "On the other hand, in stern justice, we must lay on the soul of this man, a heavy responsibility for the consummation of Negro disfranchisement, the decline of the Negro college and public school and the firmer establishment of color caste."

With Washington gone from the scene, Du Bois was regarded by many as the outstanding black leader in the United States. Yet his relationship with most NAACP board members was frequently strained in spite of his lofty status. As the months passed and the viewpoint of his editorials became evident, they sought to dissociate themselves from his opinions. Villard, never a strong supporter of the black scholar, especially disliked having Du Bois as the sole voice of the *Crisis*.

In September 1911, Du Bois wrote in the *Crisis* that blacks should arm themselves during racist attacks. "We have crawled and pleaded for justice and we have been cheerfully spat upon and murdered and burned," his editorial argued. "If we are to die, in

Few men had a more embattled relationship with Du Bois than NAACP board chairman Oswald Garrison Villard (above), who argued constantly with Du Bois that he should not have complete control over the Crisis. *Shortly after Villard tired of his battles with Du Bois and resigned from the board in 1914, his replacement, Joel Spingarn (opposite), wrote to the* Crisis *editor that people "yield to you for the reason that parents yield to spoilt children in company, for fear of creating a scene: they were less willing than you to wreck our cause before the colored world."*

God's name let us perish like men and not like bales of hay." The statement made Villard, who served as board chairman, very nervous, and he let Du Bois know about it.

Villard was also irritated by Du Bois's practice of listing the previous month's lynchings in each issue of the journal. In March 1913, he ordered Du Bois to print "a list of Negro crimes" alongside the lynching totals. Du Bois refused, prompting Villard to inform the other board members that the editor's lack of cooperation was jeopardizing the association. Du Bois later complained to Ovington that Villard "is used to advising colored men and giving them orders and he simply cannot bring himself to work with one as an equal." He knew Villard's participation in the NAACP was vitally important to its fund-raising efforts. But that was not enough to make Du Bois relinquish control of the *Crisis*. If his thinking was sometimes too forward for those around him, so be it.

In January 1914, just when the disagreements between the two men seemed ready to divide the organization, Villard resigned from the board. Joel Spingarn took his place as chairman and helped smooth things over with Du Bois, who had been insisting that some of the white board members were dragging their feet in the civil rights struggle. In early 1916, the board agreed to guarantee Du Bois absolute control over the *Crisis*.

In August of that same year, Spingarn sponsored a three-day conference at his farm in Amenia, New York, that brought together the various factions of the black rights movement. "It marks the birth of a new spirit of united purpose and effort that will have far-reaching results," the *New York Age* said of the Amenia Conference. It was an opinion that was echoed by Robert Moton (Washington's replacement as Tuskegee principal), John Hope, William Monroe Trotter, and Du Bois, who were among the more than 50 prominent black leaders in attendance.

James Weldon Johnson, a well-regarded black author and diplomat, was also there to support the Amenia resolutions, which called for higher education and complete political freedom for blacks. Four months after the conference, the NAACP named him its field secretary and gave him the responsibility of setting up additional branches and recruiting new members. Du Bois called Johnson's appointment "entirely desirable."

In December 1916, the NAACP also decided to act on Du Bois's request and publish material about the organization in a newsletter, the *Branch Bulletin*, completely freeing up the *Crisis* for broader matters. Du Bois remained the driving force behind the journal. When he entered the hospital in late 1916 and early 1917 for two operations that resulted in his losing a kidney, Spingarn wrote in the *Crisis*, "I walked out of the hospital, thinking of all that it would mean for 12 million people if this champion of theirs were not permitted to live. Others might wield brilliant pens; others would speak with something of his quiet eloquence. But never again could these millions find another leader exactly like him."

Though Spingarn and Ovington supported Du Bois, the NAACP board members who deemed him too radical spurred the editor to look outside the association and coordinate with other activist groups. Du Bois formed links with feminists, birth control advocates, socialists, and others during his first decade in New York. Greenwich Village, New York's center of cultural and intellectual life, was where he met many of the men and women interested in promoting social change.

After the turn of the century, American industries enjoyed a boom that changed the nation's entire makeup and led to the Progressive Era, a period that began in the second decade of the 20th century. Southern migrants seeking work arrived in northern industrial centers. Cities grew in population, and the influx of job seekers created a considerable number of social problems, especially in the areas of housing and labor. Socially minded intellectuals like Du Bois attempted to address these ills.

The more radical activists maintained that America's social problems were caused by a concentration of wealth in the hands of a small group of people that exploited the masses. Europe had been struggling with a similar situation for some time, and there the leaders of urban workers embraced the idea of socialism, a system in which the means of production and distribution of goods are owned and controlled by the state. Before long, several Greenwich Village activists started spreading strong socialist messages, and Du Bois listened to their arguments.

Socialism in the United States was not confined to the cities. Wherever people worked for low wages—the mines of West Virginia, the steel mills in Pittsburgh—the Socialist party took hold. By 1912, it claimed to have 118,000 members, and the steady rise in the party membership prompted Du Bois, a Republican, to reconsider his political views. For several years, he had been disenchanted with his party, which had been the traditional party of black Americans ever since the days of Abraham Lincoln. When Eugene V. Debs, the charismatic Socialist party leader, declared in 1911 that his party was a friend of the black worker, Du Bois decided to join its ranks.

Du Bois was not a radical socialist. He supported organized labor and lobbied strongly for women's rights. But he did not believe that all industries needed to be owned by the state—only those that provided essential services. Socialism, he felt, would free people from their obsession with material acquisition and allow them the opportunity to focus on spiritual and intellectual pursuits. He expressed many of these hopes in his first novel, *The Quest of the Silver Fleece*, which was published in 1911.

Nevertheless, Du Bois ended his association with the Socialist party after one year. He supported Woodrow Wilson, the Democratic nominee for president, over Debs in the 1912 election because he felt Wilson had a realistic chance of beating the incumbent president, William Howard Taft. Du Bois, as always, based his decision on the best interests of his race. Wilson had promised to appoint blacks in his administration. As it turned out, Wilson proved to be a severe disappointment to Du Bois, who never rejoined the Socialist party but remained committed to the socialist cause.

When World War I broke out in 1914, Du Bois supported the Socialist party's stand that the United States should avoid getting involved in the conflict. Party members saw the war as a struggle between crumbling European empires, with the working class serving as cannon fodder. Since his days in Berlin, Du Bois had observed the relations between European nations and their colonies, and he saw the war as an attempt by the imperial powers to exert greater control over their interests in Africa and Asia. Whites were fighting, he wrote in 1915, "to share the spoils of exploiting 'chinks and niggers.' " That same year, he published *The Negro*, a cultural and political history of the black race that discussed his views of the Pan-African movement in greater detail.

The *Crisis* covered the war extensively, and the coverage reflected Du Bois's continuing interest in Pan-Africanism. He hoped that the European empires would weaken to such an extent that their colonies would have the opportunity to rebel. But when the United States entered the war in 1917, Du Bois rejected the Socialist party's position and supported American involvement. He wrote in a *Crisis* editorial in August 1918, "This is our country: We have worked for it, we have suffered for it, we have fought for it," and added, "then this is our war."

Du Bois believed that if black Americans fought for democracy, then whites would be pressured into allowing blacks to enjoy the full benefits of democracy. In addition, he saw the war as an opportunity for black soldiers to show that they were competent and courageous and able to cooperate with whites. The army remained segregated, however, and in most cases the war did little to advance the cause of equal rights.

World War I improved the prospects of black Americans in only a few ways. Recruitment for the war effort depleted the white labor force and opened up jobs for many blacks in the industrial North. As had happened in the early 1900s, droves of blacks once again left the South for urban centers, where they became accustomed to a higher standard of living and developed advanced job skills. Moreover, the black American soldiers who fought in Europe became accustomed to cultures that did not segregate blacks—an eye-opening experience that contributed to a new sense of self-esteem among the returning troops. This rise in black expectations began to emerge after the war, especially in Harlem, which flourished as a black community in the 1920s.

For the most part, though, the end of the war brought racial strife. White troops returning from the European front in 1918 found that blacks had taken their jobs and were willing to work for less pay. These white laborers eventually expressed their discontent in vicious racial attacks during the bloody "red summer" of 1919, when race riots erupted in more than 20 cities.

Du Bois's call for blacks to close ranks and take part in the war effort was belittled by most socialists. "No intelligent Negro is willing to lay down his life for the United States as it now exists," avowed the *Messenger*, a radical journal founded by the Socialists A. Philip Randolph and Chandler Owen. They and many of their supporters viewed Du Bois as an accommodationist, much like his former rival, Booker T. Washington, had been.

A. Philip Randolph, cofounder of a radical Socialist newspaper and a much admired labor leader, often criticized the political views that Du Bois promoted in the Crisis. Yet Randolph also acknowledged that Du Bois's writings, especially The Souls of Black Folk, had convinced him at an early age that it was "absolutely necessary to fight for social equality."

Du Bois, however, was skeptical that America was ready for revolutionary changes. In Russia, where a widespread revolt had taken place in 1917, the lines in the class struggle had been clearly drawn: the workers versus the rich. An armed struggle in the United States, though, was not only impractical but objectionable. It was unreasonable to assume that white workers would join forces with black laborers and fight a class war, Du Bois argued. "We expect . . . changes to come mainly through reason, human sympathy, and the education of children," he added in a Crisis editorial, "and not by murder."

Du Bois agitated for social change in other ways. In December 1918, the NAACP sent the 50-year-old editor to the Paris Peace Conference, which got under way the following January and was supposed to settle the issues raised by War World I. Realizing that many other foreign dignitaries were gathered in France's capital city, he organized a Pan-African

Congress that met for three days in February. The 57 men and women who attended the congress issued a call for the "international protection" of all blacks: "They should be accorded the same rights as their fellow-citizens; they shall not be denied on account of race or color a voice in their own Government." Despite Du Bois's claim that the Pan-African movement acquired many influential supporters after this summit, the first Pan-African Congress, like all of its subsequent meetings, brought few substantial gains for blacks.

Du Bois returned from overseas eager to see American society embark on an era of postwar reconstruction and more generous legal measures in support of blacks—similar to what had taken place in the nation immediately after the Civil War. "We return from the slavery of the uniform which the world's madness demanded us to don to the freedom of civil garb," he wrote in the May 1919 issue of the *Crisis*, asking

Du Bois (front row, fourth from right) at a meeting in the nation's capital to discuss the federal government's employment of black soldiers during World War I. Convinced that the government was sincerely trying to address the demands of blacks, he said: "It had commissioned over seven hundred Negro officers; I had had a personal interview with Newton Baker, secretary of war, and he had made categorical promises; [President Woodrow] Wilson had spoken out against lynching; and I had myself been offered a captaincy in the Intelligence Service."

Du Bois believed that the black soldiers who participated in World War I (including the ones marching here on January 17, 1918, in celebration of the 50th anniversary of black enfranchisement) would advance the cause of black rights. "I thought that in a fight with America against militarism and for democracy we could be fighting for the emancipation of the Negro race," he said.

black Americans to "marshal every ounce of our brain and brawn to fight a sterner, longer, more unbending battle against the forces of hell in our own land. *We return. We return from fighting. We return fighting.* Make way for Democracy!"

Yet the militant tone of this *Crisis* editorial alarmed the U.S. government, which briefly stopped the May issue from being distributed through the mail. Du Bois's alleged disloyalty was then taken up by South Carolina congressman James Byrnes, who argued that the inflammatory writings of the NAACP's director of publicity and research had caused the postwar race riots. Byrnes sought unsuccessfully to indict Du Bois for espionage. Radical socialists continued to attack him as well.

Similar conflicts hounded Du Bois throughout the 1920s. "It was thus a decade of infinite effort and discouraging turmoil," he wrote in his autobiography. But he refused to have it otherwise. "I had to be a part of the revolution through which the world was going and to feel in my own soul the scars of its battles," he said.

As fate would have it, one of Du Bois's first skirmishes in the new decade was to be his most bitter struggle of all.

6

A BITTER
HARVEST

❦

IN BLACK AMERICAN history, two personal feuds tower over all others: Du Bois's disagreements with Booker T. Washington, and Du Bois's battle with Marcus Garvey.

Born on the island of Jamaica in 1887, Garvey moved to Central America when he was in his twenties and actively campaigned against the brutal treatment of immigrant workers from the West Indies. Meeting with little success, he went to London in 1912 with the hope of influencing the British government to improve its treatment of colonial workers. While in England, he began reading the works of Booker T. Washington.

Washington's autobiography, *Up from Slavery*, inspired Garvey to return to Jamaica in 1914 and form the Universal Negro Improvement Association (UNIA). This organization aimed to elevate black pride and introduce a program of educational and economic development along the lines of the Tuskegee philosophy. When the UNIA failed to take hold in Jamaica, Garvey moved to New York in 1916 and established the UNIA headquarters in Harlem.

Intent on heightening black pride, the Universal Negro Improvement Association (UNIA) held lavish parades in the streets of New York throughout the 1920s. Du Bois called the UNIA "one of the most interesting spiritual movements of the modern world" but found its leader, Marcus Garvey (middle row, third from right), "a sincere and hard-working idealist" whose methods were "bombastic, wasteful, illogical and almost illegal."

An advocate of racial separatism, UNIA leader Marcus Garvey strongly opposed the integration efforts of Du Bois and the NAACP. Garvey maintained that the Crisis *editor and his adherents "believe that the black race will become, through social contact and intercourse, so mixed up with the white race as to produce a new type, probably like Du Bois himself, which in time will be the real American."*

The UNIA promoted itself to the black public by holding conferences and sponsoring spectacular parades through the streets of Harlem. Men and women decked out in colorful blue uniforms marched proudly before thousands of onlookers thrilled by the hidden power of the black race. Garvey was a consummate showman, and he quickly captured the attention of America's largest black community. Before long, he was publishing his own black newspaper, *Negro World*; presiding over the Negro Factories Corporation, an enterprise that encouraged numerous black businesses; and running the Black Star Line, a giant shipping company owned exclusively by his black supporters. By 1919, the UNIA claimed to have 2 million members and 30 chapters around the world.

Garvey captured the attention of the black masses in a way that Du Bois never did. An emotional leader who preached a curious mixture of Pan-Africanism, black nationalism, and Tuskegee rhetoric, he was more interested in lifting the spirits of his admirers and fostering racial pride than in carrying out any plans for concrete achievements. His movement, which thrived on the widespread need among blacks for reassurance in the face of so much disillusionment, touched a deeply sensitive nerve. After only a few years in America, he rivaled Du Bois as the nation's leading black spokesman.

During the first few years of the UNIA, Du Bois and the NAACP recognized the value of Garvey's contribution to racial pride despite their uncertainty about his politics. They even helped him raise funds to get his organization off the ground. But Garvey was not supportive of the NAACP. Whether it was because Du Bois had been Washington's adversary, or because the NAACP was not an all-black organization and had ties with white philanthropists, Garvey soon began making personal attacks on Du Bois, denouncing him as a "reactionary under [the] pay of white men." He told the audience at a UNIA convention in 1920, "Negroes are big, not by the size of their pocketbook, not by the alien company they keep but by their being for their race. You cannot advocate 'close ranks' today and talk 'dark water' tomorrow; you must be a hundred percent Negro."

Garvey's actions got bolder as the 1920s progressed. Impressed by his own success, he began to promote himself as a "Black Moses" striving to lead his people back to their African homeland. The Black Star Line, in which his supporters had bought shares of stock, was supposed to assist in the transportation of blacks overseas. Although Du Bois suspected that Garvey's corporate dealings were hoodwinking the public, he remained relatively quiet on the subject in his *Crisis* editorials, believing that Garvey's popular movement would soon run out of steam.

Du Bois's public attitude toward Garvey changed in early 1922. To gain support for his Back to Africa movement, Garvey formed a strange pact with the Ku Klux Klan. As had happened several times in the past, the white supremacist organization had increased dramatically in size over a short period of time and had once again proceeded to spread its reign of terror across the country. Garvey did not support the Klan's campaign of violence. Indeed, he said, "There is no white man honest enough, sympathetic enough, humane enough, liberal enough to really take up the Negro's cause and fight it to a successful conclusion." But he believed that blacks honestly knew where they stood with the racist organization and asked its help in launching a black exodus to Africa. Klan members were "better friends of the race" than the NAACP, he said in accusing the racially integrated civil rights association of trying to destroy the black cause.

Du Bois, writing in the *Crisis*, called Garvey's association with the Klan an "unholy alliance" and

Du Bois at the NAACP convention in 1920, receiving the association's Spingarn Medal. The award, established in 1914 by board chairman Joel Spingarn, is the NAACP's highest honor.

attacked the UNIA leader himself. He described Garvey as "a little, fat Black man, ugly, but with intelligent eyes and a big head." In a subsequent editorial, Du Bois wrote: "Marcus Garvey is, without doubt, the most dangerous enemy of the Negro race in America and in the world. . . . This open ally of the Ku Klux Klan should be locked up or sent home." Garvey's caustic responses were backed by his supporters, some of whom sent death threats to the 55-year-old editor.

In the June 1924 issue of the *Messenger*, A. Philip Randolph, acting as a sort of referee, called the feud between the two men the "Heavyweight Championship Bout for Afro-American-West Indian Belt, Between Battling Du Bois and Kid Garvey."

In the end, a flurry of activities led to Garvey's downfall. Virtually the entire black press attacked him for his Klan alliance, Randolph and Chandler Owen helped form a Garvey Must Go movement, and street rallies in Harlem took up the cry. The Black Star Line, seriously mismanaged from the start, soon fell into financial ruin, and the UNIA went with it.

The final blow came in June 1923, when Garvey was convicted on mail fraud charges in connection with the Black Star enterprise. After appealing his conviction without success, he entered a federal prison in 1925. He served half of his five-year sentence and then was deported from the country. He attempted to reestablish the UNIA but garnered few supporters. Garvey died in near poverty in 1940.

For Du Bois, the worst aspect of Garvey's rise as a black leader was the effect that it had on his own Pan-African efforts. The collapse of the UNIA's black nationalist program reduced black America's interest in the development and affairs of Africa. Nevertheless, Du Bois, intent on carrying out the fight for an independent Africa, took part in three Pan-African Congresses in the 1920s: in London, Brussels, and Paris (1921), in New York (1927), and in Tunisia (1929).

Throughout the decade, Du Bois was often in transit, giving lectures, holding conferences, and setting up exhibitions. His position with the NAACP, which had unquestionably become the nation's leading antidiscriminatory organization and which had awarded him its prestigious Spingarn Award in 1920,

Throughout the 1920s, Du Bois remained a leading proponent of Pan-Africanism. At the Second Pan-African Congress, which was held in 1921 in three stages—in London, Brussels (below, with Du Bois seated second from right), and Paris—he led a call to end the domination of the African colonies by all imperial powers, especially England and Belgium.

Du Bois and his first wife, Nina, with James Weldon Johnson, who became the NAACP's executive secretary in 1920. "Du Bois in battle," Johnson said, "is a stern, bitter, relentless fighter, who, when he has put aside his sword, is among his particular friends the most jovial and fun-loving of men."

helped Du Bois remain squarely in the middle of the fray for equal rights. James Weldon Johnson, who became the association's executive secretary in 1920, and Walter White, Johnson's chief assistant, who was in charge of investigating lynchings, transformed the NAACP into an organization with a predominantly black staff.

Du Bois devoted what little free time he had to literary endeavors that complemented his editing of the *Crisis* and advanced the cause of black literature. In 1920, he published what he called a "semi-auto-biography," *Darkwater: Voices from Within the Veil.* His next book, *The Gift of Black Folk: Negroes in the Making of America*, which described black cultural achievements, was published in 1924, and *Dark Princess: A Romance* appeared four years later.

Du Bois also continued to publish his own poems and short stories in the *Crisis*, which he had been doing since the magazine's inception. He encouraged young black writers, including Jean Toomer and Countee Cullen, to contribute to the journal as well. Du Bois was remarkably selfless in his desire to see the next generation of blacks artists achieve distinction, and he did all he could to help them.

Harlem not only grew but blossomed as a black community in the 1920s, and the new spirit of racial pride was captured by the district's bold young artists and entertainers. They represented what scholar Alain Locke called the "New Negro." Daring and unfettered, they "want everything that is said about us to tell of the best and highest and noblest in us," Du Bois commented in the *Crisis*.

Du Bois contributed to the Harlem Renaissance in many ways besides his work with the *Crisis*. An annual feature of the periodical was a special children's edition, and in early 1920, with the help of coeditors Jessie Fauset and Augustus Dill, he began publishing another magazine: the *Brownies' Book*, a monthly that included stories, poems, and short biographies aimed at a young black audience. Du Bois, who professed a great love for children, appeared in each issue as a character named the Crow. "I like my black feathers—don't you?" his alter ego said suggestively to the youthful readers.

Paul Robeson, the noted actor and singer, was among Du Bois's "protégés" in Harlem, as was the poet Langston Hughes. A lover of music since his days in the Fisk Glee Club, Du Bois promoted the efforts of black singers and musicians and helped establish a black theatrical company in New York's uptown district. In addition, *Crisis* covers regularly featured the work of black artists.

Du Bois did not always agree with the trends of the Harlem Renaissance. Early in the movement's development, he criticized black artists for producing works that functioned chiefly as racial propaganda.

The nation's premier black journal, the Crisis *regularly featured the drawings and writings of America's leading black artists. Du Bois, however, contributed more material to its pages than anyone else. In addition to his editorials, the* Crisis *published his poems, short stories, and plays, including* The Star of Ethiopia, *a dramatic history of the black race that celebrated the 50th anniversary of the Emancipation Proclamation. The pageant was published in the November 1913 issue of* The Crisis *and received spectacular staging in New York that same autumn, attracting an audience of 14,000.*

Jessie Fauset (above) helped Du Bois edit the Crisis *and also worked with him on the* Brownies' Book *(opposite), a magazine for a young audience. Although the children's monthly lasted for only two years, Du Bois looked back on the project "with infinite satisfaction."*

It was important, he felt, for artists to present the world as they found it. But by the middle of the decade, he felt that black artists, especially the writer Claude McKay, had gone too far in portraying both the destitution and the caged desires of black men and women. Du Bois was afraid that such exaggerated writings would substantiate the false notions that whites held about black life, and it was out of the belief that black art should elevate the race that he wrote his second novel, *Dark Princess*, which was published in 1928.

Du Bois did not reside in Harlem during its heyday. He lived in a black housing project called the Dunbar Apartments. Years later, however, he became one of Harlem's most notable residents, settling at 409 Edgecombe Avenue, the tallest building in Sugar Hill, the district's elite neighborhood. Living nearby were Robeson, Hughes, White, and the bandleader and composer Duke Ellington. NAACP officials Roy Wilkins and Thurgood Marshall moved into the same apartment building as Du Bois in later years.

In 1928, Du Bois turned 60, and the number was of great significance to him. Although he was at an age when most people were beginning to slow down, he was ready to plow ahead. All his life he had been a man of discipline and habit. He had a well-organized daily regime that ensured he got adequate rest, he ate carefully, and he did not drink. All told, he was in excellent health and eager to help along the men and women who embodied his theory of the Talented Tenth.

Du Bois topped off 1928 with a huge celebration in Harlem: the marriage of his daughter to the poet Countee Cullen. Yolande had attended private school in London and then had followed in her father's footsteps by studying at Fisk University. Du Bois helped plan her elaborate nuptial ceremony. With Langston Hughes and the writer Arna Bontemps serving as ushers, the bride and groom entered

Du Bois (front row, right) seated next to his first wife, Nina, at their daughter Yolande's wedding in 1928. The poet Countee Cullen (middle row, center) was the bridegroom, and the writers Langston Hughes and Arna Bontemps (back row, middle) were among the ushers.

the room to a wedding march that was accompanied by the trills of live canaries in gilded cages. It was, many of the guests felt, one of the most spectacular social events that Harlem had ever witnessed.

But this era of enthusiasm and prosperity, which was capped in 1929 by the NAACP's celebration of its 20th anniversary, was not to last. On October 24, 1929, stock prices fell dramatically on the New York Stock Exchange, forcing countless businesses to close and creating widespread unemployment throughout the nation. A new period in American history soon began: the Great Depression.

In the days immediately following the stock market crash, many blacks felt that wealthy whites were the only ones who would be hurt by the event. As Hughes pointed out, "The Negro had but few pegs to fall." But it soon became clear that the Harlem Renaissance was over. By February 1930, there was "five times as much unemployment in Harlem as in other parts of the city," the *Herald Tribune* reported. Two years later, one-third of the nation was living at the poverty level, and half of Harlem's 200,000 residents were depending on relief organizations to help stem the ravaging effects of the depression.

The depression intensified Du Bois's radicalism. He filled the pages of the *Crisis* with proposals to combat the dire economic situation through the "cooperation and socialization of wealth." The black population, he said, could not expect the aid of whites during such a time of crisis. It was therefore essential that blacks pool their resources and support black enterprises. In effect, they should use racial segregation to their own advantage. Separate racial institutions did not have to mean racial discrimination.

Du Bois's call for "voluntary segregation" in the January 1934 issue of the *Crisis* greatly upset the members of the NAACP's executive board, who were

The lavish wedding reception of Du Bois's daughter, Yolande (front row, center), was one of the high points of the Harlem Renaissance, a period when a rich, new spirit emerged in the nation's largest black urban center.

Du Bois at work on the Crisis, *with coeditors Jessie Fauset (left) and Augustus Dill (standing) in the editorial offices. Du Bois was the main voice of the* Crisis *for 24 years.*

opposed to the idea of segregation in any form. None was more annoyed than Walter White, who had replaced James Weldon Johnson in 1931 as the association's executive secretary. An extremely fair-skinned black who had done extensive work for the NAACP by posing as a white man in the South, White was certainly no fan of Du Bois's. The Atlanta-born White may have been the perfect embodiment of the Talented Tenth theory, but he did not grow up with Du Bois as his mentor, and he did not agree with many of the editor's socialist doctrines.

White attacked Du Bois's position on segregation in the March 1934 issue of the *Crisis.* Moreover, he reprimanded its editor for publishing an opinion that was not backed by the association. "Let us not sit down and do nothing for self-defense and self-organization just because we are too stupid or too distrustful of ourselves to take vigorous and decisive action," Du Bois countered in picking apart White's explanation of the NAACP's stand on segregation.

But arguing was of little use. The circulation of the *Crisis* had been steadily decreasing since the late 1920s, and the journal was losing money by the time the Great Depression was well under way. "In the early days the magazine amounted to more than the organization," Mary Ovington had told Du Bois in 1930, and she went on to warn him that the day would come when "the *Crisis* would either disappear or become distinctly an NAACP organ, and that means it must be under the secretary."

On May 21, 1934, that day arrived. The NAACP's board of directors voted that "the *Crisis* is the organ of the Association and no salaried officer of the Association shall criticize the policy, work, or officers of the Association in the pages of the *Crisis*." Upon hearing their verdict, Du Bois promptly resigned from his editorial post. The board refused to accept his resignation for several months but finally relented in late June.

Du Bois had founded the *Crisis* and had kept it influential for 24 years. As the NAACP said in announcing his resignation: "He created, what never existed before, a Negro intelligentsia, and many who have never read a word of his writings are his spiritual disciples and descendants. Without him the Association could never have been what it was and is." Nevertheless, he had been pressured into leaving the journal in the hands of an organization whose leaders, as he put it, "have neither the ability or the disposition to guide it in the right direction." That act of relinquishment, he wrote in *Dusk of Dawn*, "was like giving up a child."

7

THE STRUGGLE
FOR PEACE

Du BOIS'S GOOD FRIEND John Hope came
to the rescue. Hope, who had become president of a
revamped Atlanta University in 1929, asked the 66-
year-old Du Bois to return to the South and become
chairman of the university's Department of Sociology. Du Bois accepted the offer under one condition:
that the position was for life. His income had always
been low—indeed, he had earned only $5,000 a year
during his last 18 years with the NAACP—and he
needed the security of a steady job.

His wife, Nina, was not as enthusiastic about
returning to Atlanta. She associated the city with
the loss of their first child and the brutal 1906 Atlanta
race riots. She elected to move instead to Baltimore,
where her daughter, Yolande, whose marriage to
Countee Cullen had ended in divorce a few years
earlier, was a well-established schoolteacher. Despite
living apart from Nina, Du Bois later said of his marriage: "It was not an absolutely ideal union, but it
was happier than most."

*Du Bois at the NAACP convention in 1941, at the time when he
was working to have Atlanta, Fisk, and Howard Universities join
with the nation's black land-grant colleges to undertake a wide-
ranging study on black American life. His plan, patterned after the
Atlanta University studies he launched nearly a half century earlier, was approved the following year.*

Du Bois at home and on vacation: standing in front of his house in Baltimore, Maryland (above); and relaxing at Camp Litchfield, Maine (opposite).

As soon as Du Bois arrived in Atlanta in 1934, he resumed the wide-ranging studies that he had abandoned when he joined the NAACP. In addition to these research projects, he taught graduate courses and founded a new journal, *Phylon*, which focused on issues in social science. He also wrote articles and columns for several black newspapers, including the *Pittsburgh Courier* and New York's *Amsterdam News*, and produced several important books.

The first of these works to reach the public was *Black Reconstruction: An Essay Toward a History of the Part Which Black Folk Played in the Attempt to Reconstruct Democracy in America, 1860-1880*. Published in 1935, it was soon regarded as one of Du Bois's most valuable works of scholarship. Walter White went so far as to send a copy to First Lady Eleanor Roosevelt with the hope that it would add to her understanding of the South's racial problems. "The slave went free; stood a brief moment in the sun; then moved back again toward slavery," Du Bois wrote in *Black Reconstruction* in summation of the black American's plight since the Civil War.

In 1935, Du Bois also published an essay entitled "A Negro Nation Within the Nation." It was one of his most hard-hitting pieces. "The colored people of America are coming to face the fact quite simply that most white Americans do not like them, and are planning neither for their survival, nor for their definite future," he stated.

The following year, Du Bois took the time to compare the pros and cons of American society with the world at large. Backed by a grant to study foreign educational systems, he spent seven months abroad, traveling from Germany and Austria to the Soviet Union, China, and Japan. He spent most of his trip, however, observing the rapidly changing political scene in global politics. He witnessed the rise of Chancellor Adolf Hitler in Germany, where the white racist philosophy of his Nazi party was visibly rearing its ugly head. Du Bois reported in a December 1936 newspaper column that the Nazis' policies were "an attack on civilization, comparable only to such horrors as the Spanish Inquisition and the African slave trade."

The Soviet Union, on the other hand, left Du Bois deeply impressed. He had visited the country 10 years earlier and had found it filled with "a suppressed mass of poor, working people—people as ignorant, poor, superstitious and cowed as my own American Negroes—so lifted in hope and starry-eyed with new determination." Despite the absence of color caste in Russia, he did not believe that its brand of communism would work in the United States.

Du Bois had never seriously considered joining the American Communist party. But his trip to the Soviet Union in 1936 altered his political views somewhat. "The only hope of humanity today lies in . . . the common interests of the working class," he wrote upon returning to Atlanta. The following year, he moved one step closer to admitting the value of Soviet doctrines. "I am not a communist but I appreciate what the communists are trying to do," he said.

In 1939, Du Bois published *Black Folk Then and Now: An Essay in the History and Sociology of the Negro Race*, a work much along the lines of his 1915 book, *The Negro*. His views on the future of mankind and his personal creed were eloquently put forth the next year in an autobiographical work, *Dusk of Dawn*. The 72-year-old author's examination of his own life—a change of pace from his books on the life of other blacks—allowed him to explain "the problem of color" in depth.

Dusk of Dawn also gave Du Bois the opportunity to clarify his views on voluntary segregation. He insisted that he was still totally against the idea of black nationalism. "Full Negro rights and Negro equality in America" remained his "ultimate object." Indeed, he felt the time was ripe for great changes in American society.

With the eruption of World War II in late 1939, the 1940s was destined to be a decade of political confrontation and social upheaval. "If Hitler wins, down with the blacks!" Du Bois observed in a 1941 article he wrote for the *Amsterdam News*. "If the democracies win, the blacks are already down." Those two choices could be improved, he said, if the United States was to win the war and expand its fight for democracy to the area within its own borders.

While Du Bois was helping to find a way out of the chaos of the war, he found himself in the middle of another bitter feud. Florence Read, the president of Spellman College, the sister school of Atlanta University, disliked his emphasis on black studies and was wary of his political radicalism; she thought it discouraged white patrons from supporting the college. She also opposed his resumption of the Atlanta conferences and fought against the publication of the *Phylon* quarterly. In November 1943, she led a movement to retire Du Bois from the faculty.

Du Bois had been hired by John Hope with the understanding that his spot at the university was for life. But Hope had died in 1936, and the school's board of trustees invoked a provision that required all professors to retire when they reached the age of 65. "Without a word of warning," Du Bois recalled in his autobiography, "I found myself at the age of 76 without employment and with less than $5,000 of savings."

The blow was softened somewhat by a suprising offer to return to the NAACP. Walter White, in offering Du Bois the position of director of special research, was willing to put aside his personal differences with the former *Crisis* editor. The executive secretary recognized the value of Du Bois's international reputation and wanted him to write documents and speeches as well as make a few public appearances on behalf of the association.

In September 1944, Du Bois returned to the NAACP. But he soon made it clear that he refused to serve merely as "window dressing." When he joined White and educator Mary McLeod Bethune as consultants to the United States delegation at the founding of the United Nations in 1945, he campaigned vigorously for an end to colonial rule. He continued his fight for Pan-Africanism that October, when he traveled to Manchester, England, to take part in the fifth Pan-African Congress. He also wrote about African affairs in *Color and Democracy: Colonies and Peace*, which was published in 1945, and *The World and Africa: An Inquiry into the Part Which Africa Has Played in World History*, which appeared two years later.

Much to White's surprise, the elderly Du Bois became increasingly involved in NAACP activities. Before long, the differences between the two men surfaced yet again. The troubles began literally in Du Bois's office. The NAACP refused to give him any work space, forcing him to pay for his office accommodations out of his own pocket. He had to buy his own furniture and supplies as well.

The seriousness of the problems between Du Bois and White soon escalated, with the NAACP chief objecting to the former *Crisis* editor's involvement in a variety of endeavors. By the time Du Bois refused White's request to draft several memorandums for a 1948 Human Rights Commission meeting, which the executive secretary was planning to attend, the battle lines were drawn. Du Bois believed that the meeting was his concern, not White's. "Surely," Du Bois said later, "in my nearly 50 years of work for the American Negro I had earned the right to some small niche

"I returned to the NAACP after an absence of ten years during which I had not followed closely its development," Du Bois said after reuniting with the association in 1944. *"The results astonished me. The income had quadrupled, the membership approached a half-million; the staff had tripled or more. It had become a big business, smoothly run and extraordinarily influential."* Two things there had not changed, however. Executive secretary Walter White and board of directors member Mary Ovington were still two of the most influential people in the NAACP.

where I could think and act with reasonable free-dom."

Du Bois apparently overstepped the line when he sent White a combative memo. The note stated that Du Bois was eager to know what his exact responsibilities in the association were. It also outlined many of his complaints with the current NAACP policies. The association's board responded to the memo by dismissing the 80-year-old Du Bois from his post.

Another old friend came immediately to Du Bois's aid, much as had happened when he left the NAACP 14 years earlier. Paul Robeson, the noted singer and actor who had become an outspoken supporter of the poor and the oppressed, asked Du Bois to become honorary vice-chairman of the Council on African Affairs, a group dedicated to assisting African nationalists. It was an organization that the U.S. government regarded as subversive.

In 1938, the U.S. House of Representatives had formed the House Un-American Activities Committee (HUAC) to investigate the affairs of U.S. citizens whom the government suspected of acting against American interests. The committee was supposed to stop the flow of Communist propaganda that was feeding the public's fear of the Soviet Union, which was growing rapidly as an international power. But by the mid-1940s, the committee was prying into the life of anyone whom it suspected of being a radical. The Federal Bureau of Investigation (FBI) did most of the legwork for this feverish witch-hunt, which was fully sanctioned by the government.

In 1949, Du Bois attended peace conferences both in the United States and abroad that were organized by the kind of people whom American authorities regarded as dangerous. He flirted even more closely with the "red menace" in 1950, when he became chairman of the Peace Information Center, an outfit that the U.S. Department of Justice regarded as part of the Soviet Union's propaganda machine. That July, the FBI quietly began to collect evidence against the Peace Information Center.

Du Bois's wife, Nina, died in Baltimore that same month. She had suffered a stroke five years earlier and had remained an invalid ever since. Du Bois buried her in Great Barrington, next to their son, Burghardt, bringing to a close a marriage that had lasted for more than 50 years.

When Du Bois returned to New York in the summer of 1950, the American Labor party asked him to be its candidate for the U.S. Senate in the November elections. Although he knew he had little chance of winning, he strongly believed that America needed a third political group to offset the Democratic and Republican parties, which he thought had very

In 1948, Du Bois became honorary vice-chairman of the Council on African Affairs, an African nationalist group of which his longtime friend, singer and actor Paul Robeson (left), was a member. "It had been the dream of idealists . . . that the stain of American slavery would eventually be wiped out by the service which American descendants of African slaves would render Africa," Du Bois said.

similar platforms. He readily agreed to run for office and help promote the American Labor party.

Du Bois also knew that his candidacy would give him a good opportunity to air his views before the public. "I wondered if a series of plain talks in a political campaign would not be my last and only chance to tell the truth as I saw it," he wrote in *In Battle for Peace: The Story of My 83rd Birthday*, which was published in 1952. He was received warmly wherever he spoke on the campaign trail, and he ultimately received more than 200,000 votes on election day—a strong show of support in what was, as he had predicted, a losing cause.

Du Bois was backed in his bid for the Senate by Shirley Graham, who had first met him when she was 13 years old and had later been one of his graduate

Du Bois during his campaign for the U.S. Senate in 1950. Although he lost the election, his candidacy put him back in the public spotlight and enabled his political messages to reach a large number of people.

On Valentine's Day, 1951, Du Bois, at the age of 82, weds Shirley Graham, his longtime aide. She later said that when they first discussed their marriage plans, "he reiterated that he was 'selfish' and 'too old,' but he didn't act old!"

students at Atlanta University. A widow who was 40 years his junior, she was deeply involved in black political affairs and remained in close contact with her former teacher. After much effort, she succeeded in persuading Du Bois that her help and companionship would be a big boost to him, and they were married on Valentine's Day in 1951.

At first, they kept the marriage a secret, because Du Bois wanted to protect his new bride. Five days before the wedding, on February 9, the federal government indicted the Peace Information Center for failing to register as an agent of the Soviet Union. The indictment named five defendants as felons, each of whom faced a possible five-year prison sentence. One of the people singled out for defying the authority of the U.S. government was Du Bois.

The trial began on November 8, 1951, in Washington, D.C., and attracted attention all over the world. The Department of Justice pursued the case

Du Bois stands outside the federal courthouse in Washington, D.C., in February 1951, waiting to be arraigned on the charge that the Peace Information Center, of which he was chairman, had failed to register as "an agent of a foreign principal." With him are his second wife, Shirley (second from right), and three of his co-defendants.

as if it were a show trial, which in actuality it was. Du Bois, at the age of 83, was handcuffed to a fellow defendant and searched for concealed weapons. A bailiff removed the handcuffs only after the press had taken photos of the submissive black leader.

As the trial proceeded, it soon became clear that the prosecution had absolutely no proof that the literature distributed by the Peace Information Center was connected with the Soviet Union. Du Bois and his codefendants were acquitted eight days after the court proceedings began. Nevertheless, the trial left him a marked man.

In February 1952, Du Bois and his wife applied to the State Department for visas to travel to Brazil, where a peace conference was to be held. "Your proposed travel would be contrary to the best interests of the United States," the department responded in denying travel documents to them. But the couple refused to give up. Shortly thereafter, they flew to Toronto to attend the Canadian Peace Congress. Yet they never set foot outside the Toronto airport. U.S. officials immediately put them on a plane back to America.

Du Bois was outraged. A federal court had acquitted him of any wrongdoing, yet he was still treated like a criminal. He had traveled all his life, but he was now no longer permitted to go abroad.

Upon returning to the United States, Du Bois continued to be harassed. The FBI tampered with his mail. The police interrogated his neighbors about visitors to the Du Bois residence. Publishers stopped asking him for articles. Universities no longer invited him to lecture.

Day by day, Du Bois's influence on black affairs diminished, until his voice of protest was almost completely silenced. "I lost my leadership of my race," he bemoaned. "The colored children ceased to hear my name." ❦

A rare sight to foreign customs officials in the 1950s: Du Bois's passport photograph. The U.S. government refused to let him travel abroad from 1952 to 1958 and again in 1959 because of his alleged ties with Communist nations.

8

THE FATHER
OF AFRICA

I T WAS A bitter experience and I bowed before the storm," Du Bois said of the outcast status that was conferred on him in 1952. "But I did not break." As the U.S. government's witch-hunt for Communists continued in the early 1950s, he turned his attention away from articles of protest and addressed black issues in works of fiction.

In 1957, Du Bois published his third novel, *The Ordeal of Mansart*, which became the first volume in his *Black Flame* trilogy. Manuel Mansart, the main character in the book, is an intellectual who heads a black college in Georgia in the late 1800s and comes face-to-face with racial violence. The subsequent volumes in the trilogy—*Mansart Builds a School* and *Worlds of Color*, published in 1959 and 1961, respectively—follow the story of the Mansart clan up to the 1960s and conclude with the emergence of Africa as a world power. All told, the trilogy offers a clear indication that Du Bois was losing hope in America as a place where blacks could live freely.

Consequently, it was to Du Bois's great surprise and deep regret that he was forced to remain on the sidelines in the 1950s when huge advances in the civil rights struggle came to pass. The first major victory took place in May 1954, when the U.S. Supreme Court ruled unanimously in the case of *Brown v. Board of Education* that "separate educational facilities are inherently unequal . . . segregation is a denial of the equal protection of the laws." Du Bois

Beginning in mid-1958, Du Bois and his second wife, Shirley, spent five months in the Soviet Union. "The ideal of every American is the millionaire—or at least the man of 'independent' means of income," he said. "The Soviet Union, on the contrary, is seeking to make a nation believe that work, and work that is hard and in some respects even disagreeable, and to a large extent physical, is a necessity of human life at present."

Soviet Union premier Nikita Khrushchev greets Du Bois and his wife in Moscow. During their talks, Khrushchev was struck by Du Bois's suggestion that the Soviets found a center to study African culture and politics, and an Institute on Africa was established in Moscow shortly thereafter.

was elated. "I have seen the impossible happen!" he exclaimed.

Nevertheless, Du Bois knew that blacks still had a long way to go before they achieved racial equality. Landmark rulings such as the *Brown* decision were a big step forward for black Americans, as were the mass protests and boycotts led by civil rights activist Martin Luther King, Jr. But, Du Bois noted pointedly, "we are not free yet."

Du Bois had even less freedom than most blacks. The State Department had asked him in 1953 to testify whether he was or had ever been a Communist. The government refused to issue him a new passport when he failed to respond. "As a matter of fact, I was not a member of that party," he later wrote in his autobiography. "Yet I refused to make any statement on the ground that the government had no legal right to question me concerning my political beliefs."

Du Bois's low status in the United States was in complete contrast to the esteem he received in Africa. It was pointed out that the one American whom all Africans had heard of was Du Bois. To most Africans, including Kwame Nkrumah, who became prime minister of the Republic of Ghana in 1957, Du Bois was "the Father of Pan-Africanism."

As new civil rights leaders emerged in the United States and he had increasingly less say in black affairs, Du Bois became even more anxious to travel to Africa and other locations. He soon got his chance. In 1958, the U.S. Supreme Court ruled that the State Department lacked the authority to demand political statements from American citizens prior to issuing them a passport. Du Bois and his wife received their

Du Bois during a visit in April 1959 with Mao Tse-tung, leader of the People's Republic of China. Upon Du Bois's return from the Communist country, the U.S. State Department seized his passport to prevent him from traveling to foreign lands that the federal government considered a threat to American interests.

travel documents that July and left the country the following month. It was his 15th trip overseas, and it lasted until the following July.

A five-month stay in the Soviet Union led Du Bois to comment that the Communist nation seemed "the only European country where people are not taught and encouraged to despise and look down on some class, group or race." The Soviets certainly did not look down on Du Bois. He received an honorary doctorate from Moscow University and the Lenin Peace Prize, one of the nation's highest honors. He also held talks with Soviet premier Nikita Khrushchev.

Du Bois then traveled to the People's Republic of China, where he noted that "China has no rank or classes." The highlight of his 10-week visit to the Eastern Communist nation was a meeting with party chairman Mao Tse-tung. "You are no darker than I am," Mao pointed out to Du Bois. "Who could tell which one of us is darker?"

Shortly after Du Bois returned to the United States in the summer of 1959, the government once again restricted his freedom to travel. The State Department confiscated his passport because of his visit to a dangerous country, "Red China," and did not return it until the following year. By then, the 91-year-old Du Bois was invigorated by his encounters in noncapitalist societies. They inspired him with visions of what might be possible in a developing land where the evils of democracy had not yet taken hold: Africa.

Nkrumah was inaugurated as the first president of Ghana in July 1960, and Du Bois was quick to attend the festivities. A short time later, Nkrumah asked Du Bois to consider moving to Ghana and starting an *Encyclopedia Africana*. "Such a study as you would conduct," the African leader said, "will open the eyes of Africans, will lay bare all the potentialities of this

Kwame Nkrumah, president of Ghana, toasts Du Bois on his 95th birthday. Du Bois had moved to Accra, the capital of Ghana, in October 1961.

vast continent, will uncover its past and will relate that past to the present. The study will be a major factor in uniting us culturally, economically and psychologically."

Du Bois was enthralled by the proposition. It would be the summation of the dreams that had sustained him through many years of disappointment. He returned to the United States and began to lay the groundwork for the encyclopedia by contacting the leading research bodies and scholars in America and abroad.

While engaged in the early stages of the planning, Du Bois received word that his daughter had died of a heart attack. The loss of Yolande convinced him that there was virtually nothing left for him in Amer-

Du Bois's state funeral (above and opposite), which took place in Accra in August 1963. He was buried just outside the Ghanian Government House.

ica. He proceeded to write to Nkrumah, offering to relocate to Ghana and oversee the entire project from a post in Africa. "My great-grandfather was carried away in chains from the Gulf of Guinea," he said after his arrival. "I have returned that my dust shall mingle with the dust of my forefathers."

But before Du Bois left the United States for good, he made one last grand gesture. On October 1, 1961, he joined the American Communist party. "Capitalism cannot reform itself; it is doomed to self-destruction. No universal selfishness can bring social good to all," he said in explaining his decision to become a party member. "Communism—the effort to give all men what they need and to ask of each the best they can contribute—this is the only way of human life."

Du Bois worked on the *Encyclopedia Africana* from his base in Accra, the capital city of Ghana, throughout 1962 and into early 1963. When his passport expired and the American consulate in Ghana refused to renew it because he was now a member of the Communist party, he renounced his U.S. citizenship and became a Ghanian citizen. To many in Africa, he was "Ghana's first citizen" and "Africa's father." His house was filled with a succession of writers and statesmen from newly independent African states, all of whom wanted him to visit their country.

Nkrumah was among those who came to see the celebrated scholar. In late August 1963, the president visited Du Bois after receiving word that he was ill. Upon seeing each other, the two men became full of emotion, well aware that the end was drawing near for the elderly Du Bois. When Nkrumah finally rose to leave, Du Bois grasped his hand and said, "I want to thank you for all you've done to make the ending of my life bountiful and beautiful. . . . Good-bye! And bless you!"

Du Bois died later that evening, on August 27, 1963. He was 95 years old. "Ghana honored him in death as she had honored him in life," Shirley, his widow, wrote, "burying him as they would have bur-

Du Bois receiving an honorary degree from the University of Ghana. "Dr. Du Bois was not only an intellectual giant exploring the frontiers of knowledge, he was in the first place a teacher," said civil rights leader Martin Luther King, Jr. "He would have wanted his life to teach us something about our tasks of emancipation."

ied a head of state." The United States was the only nation with a consulate in Ghana that did not send a representative to his funeral.

The day after Du Bois's death, 250,000 people assembled in Washington, D.C., and marched to the Lincoln Memorial in a huge show of unity for the civil rights movement. A. Philip Randolph kicked off the March on Washington by declaring to the crowd, "Let the nation and the world know the meaning of our numbers," and Martin Luther King, Jr., closed the day's events by offering his grand vision of American society. "I have a dream today!" he told the many demonstrators.

At some point during the proceedings, the news spread that W. E. B. Du Bois had died. Roy Wilkins,

who had succeeded Walter White as executive secretary of the NAACP, reminded the crowd: "At the
dawn of the twentieth century his was the voice that
was calling to you to gather here today in this cause."
One woman subsequently remarked that Du Bois was
like Moses, a great leader who never lived to see the
promised land.

King himself gave his last major address at a gath-
ering to honor the 100th anniversary of Du Bois's
birth. "Dr. Du Bois recognized that the keystone in
the arch of oppression was the myth of inferiority,
and he dedicated his brilliant talents to demolish it,"
King told an audience in New York's Carnegie Hall.
"He saw and loved progressive humanity in all its
hues, black, white, yellow, red, and brown. . . . Dr.
Du Bois has left us but he has not died. The spirit
of freedom is not buried in the grave of the valiant."

But it was, fittingly enough, Du Bois himself—
ever the eloquent black spokesman—who had the
last say on his long and remarkably productive life.
Realizing in June 1957 that each day might be his
last, he wrote down what he said was his final message
to the world. Du Bois's farewell, read to the crowd
at his funeral in Accra, concluded with the following
words:

> I have loved my work, I have loved people and my play,
> but always I have been uplifted by the thought that what
> I have done well will live long and justify my life; that what
> I have done ill or never finished can now be handed on to
> others for endless days to be finished, perhaps better than
> I could have done.
>
> And that peace will be my applause.
>
> One thing alone I charge you. As you live, believe in
> life! Always human beings will live and progress to greater,
> broader and fuller life.
>
> The only possible death is to lose belief in this truth
> simply because the great end comes slowly, because time is
> long.
>
> Good-bye.

APPENDIX

———— ❧ ————

BOOKS BY W. E. B. DU BOIS

1896   *The Suppression of the African Slave-Trade to the United States of America, 1638–1870*

1899   *The Philadelphia Negro: A Social Study*

1903   *The Souls of Black Folk: Essays and Sketches*

1909   *John Brown*

1911   *The Quest of the Silver Fleece: A Novel*

1915   *The Negro*

1920   *Darkwater: Voices from Within the Veil*

1924   *The Gift of Black Folk: Negroes in the Making of America*

1928   *Dark Princess: A Romance*

1930   *Africa—Its Place in Modern History; Africa—Its Geography, People and Products*

1935   *Black Reconstruction: An Essay Toward a History of the Part Which Black Folk Played in the Attempt to Reconstruct Democracy in America, 1860–1880*

1939   *Black Folk Then and Now: An Essay in the History and Sociology of the Negro Race*

1940   *Dusk of Dawn: An Essay Toward an Autobiography of a Race Concept*

1945   *Color and Democracy: Colonies and Peace*

1947   *The World and Africa: An Inquiry into the Part Which Africa Has Played in World History*

1952   *In Battle for Peace: The Story of My 83rd Birthday, With Comment by Shirley Graham*

1957   *The Ordeal of Mansart*

1959   *Mansart Builds a School*

1961   *Worlds of Color*

1963   *An ABC of Color: Selections from over a Half Century of the Writings of W. E. B. Du Bois*

1968   *The Autobiography of W. E. B. Du Bois: A Soliloquy on Viewing My Life from the Last Decade of Its First Century.*

CHRONOLOGY

1868   Born William Edward Burghardt Du Bois on February 23 in Great Barrington, Massachusetts

1884   Graduates as valedictorian from Great Barrington High School

1888   Graduates as valedictorian from Fisk University

1890   Graduates cum laude with a bachelor of arts degree from Harvard College

1891   Receives master of arts degree from Harvard University

1892   Begins two years of study at Friedrich Wilhelm University in Berlin, Germany

1894   Joins the faculty at Wilberforce University

1896   Receives doctorate from Harvard University; marries Nina Gomer; Du Bois becomes assistant instructor at University of Pennsylvania

1897   Son, Burghardt, is born; Du Bois becomes professor at Atlanta University; organizes the Atlanta University Studies of the Negro Problem

1899   Son, Burghardt, dies

1900   Du Bois attends first Pan-African Congress; daughter, Yolande, is born

1905   Forms the Niagara Movement

1905   Founds and edits the *Moon*

1907   Founds and edits the *Horizon*

1909   Helps found the National Association for the Advancement of Colored People (NAACP)

1910   Becomes the NAACP's director of publicity and research; founds and edits the *Crisis*

1920   Awarded the NAACP's Spingarn Medal

1934   Resigns from the *Crisis* and the NAACP board; rejoins the Atlanta University faculty

1940   Founds and edits *Phylon*

1944   Becomes director of special research for the NAACP

1948   Resigns from NAACP post; becomes chairman of Council on African Affairs

1950   First wife, Nina, dies; Du Bois campaigns for the U.S. Senate

1951   Marries Shirley Graham; Du Bois, as officer of the Peace Information Center, is indicted and acquitted on the charge of "failure to register as agent of a foreign principal"

1960   Daughter, Yolande, dies

1961   Du Bois joins the American Communist party; moves to Ghana

1963   Dies in Accra, Ghana, on August 27

FURTHER READING

Aptheker, Herbert, ed. *Annotated Bibliography of the Published Writings of W. E. B. Du Bois.* Millwood, NY: Kraus-Thomson, 1973.

———, ed. *The Correspondence of W. E. B. Du Bois.* 3 vols. Amherst: University of Massachusetts Press, 1973–78.

———, ed. *Creative Writings by W. E. B. Du Bois: A Pageant, Poems, Short Stories, and Playlets.* White Plains, NY: Kraus-Thomson, 1985.

———, ed. *The Literary Legacy of W. E. B. Du Bois.* White Plains, NY: Kraus-Thomson, 1989.

———, ed. *Writings in Periodicals Edited by W. E. B. Du Bois: Selections from the "Crisis."* 2 vols. Millwood, NY: Kraus-Thomson, 1983.

Broderick, Francis L. *W. E. B. Du Bois: Negro Leader in a Time of Crisis.* Stanford: Stanford University Press, 1959.

Butler, B. N. "Booker T. Washington, W. E. B. Du Bois, Black Americans and the NAACP." *Crisis* 85 (August 1978): 222–30.

Du Bois, Shirley Graham. *His Day Is Marching On: A Memoir of W. E. B. Du Bois.* Philadelphia: Lippincott, 1971.

Foner, Philip S. *W. E. B. Du Bois Speaks: Speeches and Addresses.* 2 vols. New York: Pathfinder Press, 1988.

Lester, Julius, ed. *The Seventh Son: The Thought and Writings of W. E. B. Du Bois.* 2 vols. New York: Random House, 1971.

Marable, Manning. *W. E. B. Du Bois: Black Radical Democrat.* Boston: Twayne Publishers, 1986.

Rampersad, Arnold. *The Art and Imagination of W. E. B. Du Bois.* Cambridge: Harvard University Press, 1976.

Rudwick, Elliott. *W. E. B. Du Bois: Voice of the Black Protest Movement.* Urbana: University of Illinois Press, 1982.

INDEX

PICTURE CREDITS

———— ❧ ————

Archives and Manuscripts, University Library, University of Massachusetts at Amherst: pp. 2, 10, 16, 21, 23, 25, 28, 32, 40, 43, 49, 56, 58, 59, 61, 66, 70, 71, 78, 79, 85, 90, 91, 92, 96, 97, 100, 101, 102, 103, 107, 108, 109, 110, 111, 112, 114, 115, 117, 118, 119, 120; Atlanta University Archives: pp. 52; The Bettmann Archive: pp. 36, 63; Fisk University: pp. 13, 33; Harvard University Archives: pp. 39, 64; Library of Congress: p. 3; Schomberg Center, New York Public Library: pp. 15, 18, 22, 27, 30, 35, 46, 54, 69, 73, 75, 76, 83, 84, 86, 87, 88, 93, 94, 95, 98, 105

MARK STAFFORD holds a master of arts degree from the University of Edinburgh in Scotland. Formerly a journalist and magazine editor in the United Kingdom, he now lives in New York City, where he works for a major book publishing company.

NATHAN IRVIN HUGGINS is W.E.B. Du Bois Professor of History and Director of the W.E.B. Du Bois Institute for Afro-American Research at Harvard University. He previously taught at Columbia University. Professor Huggins is the author of numerous books, including *Black Odyssey: The Afro-American Ordeal in Slavery*, *The Harlem Renaissance*, and *Slave and Citizen: The Life of Frederick Douglass*.